Conned Under Capitalism
How the Real World Works
For Children and Adults who behave Like Children

Dedication to the Legal profession

It is difficult being a Lawyer in the West…When you have to defend criminals who you know to be guilty and lock up the innocent because you have failed to defend then properly

How you have to lie to the Jury of 12 men and women who are clueless about the law or know how to evaluate evidence

How you never present all the evidence and selectively use evidence to support your case. How the previous convictions of your client are not revealed to the jury

How you frame questions so that witnesses can never give a full answer. Endless legal arguments over minor issues to prolong the case and add to the legal bill

Witnesses treated as criminals to undermine their testimony

Legal jargon to confuse the jury and word games with the Judge

The law of the people

Without laws there would be anarchy. The recent invasions by America into Iraq and Libya have led to collapse in law and order and infighting between different groups…War lords causing mayhem and destruction. In the DRC in Africa breakdown of law and order for over 20 years has led to civil war…many deaths and destruction…a failed state unable to protect its people

Warning…There is one law for the rich and one for the 'poor'…so it's better to be rich than poor...you get to make the laws

Around 10,000 years ago when people began to live in small communities. To live together there had to be some rules…laws…which would applicable to everyone
Tribal leader = law giver

The first law was for murder…you could be killed for murdering someone...especially relevant if someone is having an affair with your wife...that person 'needs' to die
Murder = justice = legal murder

A lot of our laws come from Religion and most our problems…if all the laws of religion were applied today, we would have a dangerous...uncivilized…barbaric population...be-headings...killing for adultery...rape would be legalized…stoning…beating children...domestic violence...covering women from head to toe...not allowed out in public...murder of gays...Lesbians...Apostates and non-believers

God's laws = murder + rape + domestic violence +land theft + child abuse

The democracy loving Greeks (plus slavery) were the first people to have a constitutional rights enshrined in 12 tables...citizens' rights...despite this it did not save the Empire.

Greek Democracy for = citizens only – excludes women and slaves

In China Confucius...who's people were very confused...gave his people a mixture of Daoism...Legalism and Confucianism...this probably explains why stir fry is so popular in China.

Laws exist to protect people and property...and act as a deterrent against injustice...not so in practice... laws to govern and facilitate trade were enacted...but not for the Empire subjects...they had no rights to protect them from exploitation

After the decline of the Greek and Roman Empire...Europe went to normality...barbaric state...it was law by trial...people were subject to inhumane and degrading treatment...if they recovered, they were considered innocent...drowning was popular...if you did not survive you were innocent

The Church banned trial by order...but duels continued. The Magna Carta is the first document to give people basic rights...followed by the English civil war and separation of power from the crown to Parliament...unfortunately Charles I lost his head...a small price for freedom

After the French Revolution...which was a bread riot...the poor could not afford their daily bread...the 'cost of living crises has been with us for a long time'. Frances's declaration of rights...excluded its colonial subjects. It took over 100 years to abolish slavery and women only got the vote after throwing themselves under the King's Horses in Little Old England.

Industrialization and organised labour in the form of Unions were able to get legislation passed for better pay and working conditions. With 'Democracy' came a legal system with checks and balances to stop abuse of power...not so in the colonies

After World War one and two...came the United Nations and its charter...while most of the world was still colonised. As I write... Israel is committing genocide against a defenceless civilian population in Gaza...the so-called defenders of democracy and human rights actively supporting the Democratic terrorist state of Israel.

It would seem international laws are applied selectively by the West...the majority world has been quick to point out the hypocrisy and double standards...opinions have not changed...there is active pressure some European countries and the USA to not bring genocide charges against Netanyahu of Israel
(Source:dk publishing the law)

In the beginning
Humans are social animals...some more social than others. In the past people lived in tribal communities...rules were based on customs...social norms and religion.

Religion is the foundation of many legal systems in the world...God gave Moses the Torah and the right to charge interest to non-Jews...later these God's laws became the Talmud...Jewish laws...which allowed even more land theft and murder in Palestine and charging of interest

In China rulers used the 'Divine right to rule'...mandate from heaven to commit unspeakable acts of murder...rape...torture and land theft...on a helpless peasant population...China is governed by three principles:

1)**Confucianism**...virtue...respect...don't be a trouble maker

2)**Daoism**...living in harmony with nature...don't be a trouble maker

3)**Legalism**...harsh rules imposed by even harsher rulers...don't be a trouble maker

After 250 years of wars within China...with the loss of millions of lives...a legally enforceable dynasty emerged which did not last

While in Athens people got the vote and slaves to abuse. Plato argued for a wise dictator with even wiser council for advice...the best form of government
Dictator democracy = council of advisors = laws = imposed on the people

Aristotle wanted a constitutional government and legislation…they ended up with neither...constant wars with bad neighbours finished of the Greek Empire...the only thing we have now in Greece is ...Greek Kebabs and Coffee and a bankrupt country

The Romans got rid of the Tyrant Superbus (it's true that's his real name) ...created a republic with two elected consuls plus an assortment of rights of the people. Emperor Constantine a Christian convert...advocated religious tolerance but not for Jews...they were persecuted relentlessly in the Roman Empire. The Christian religion forms the basis of the Western legal system...and has been imposed on the rest of the world through Colonialism

The book of Exodus...**first legal basis for retaliation**…eye for an eye for Israel this means genocidal massacres of innocent defenceless population of Gaza and the West bank…backed by the US and its vassal state the EU

About six thousand years ago the Sumerians lived in small settlements...as the numbers increased... as did the number of laws to settle disputes and Lawyers to circumvent them...cities expanded as did the number of laws to govern them…a never-ending cycle

Initially laws were word of mouth...oral tradition...King Ur had a really bad memory (like Joe Biden-ex US President) and decided things should be written down on clay tablets. King Hammurabi went one better laws were written on 7.5 feet stone pillars...with the opening declaration...King ordered by God to rule the land and get rid of wickedness and evil doers from the State…and defend the strong from the weak...So…don't be an evil doer…stay safe

The concept of 'eye for an eye'…was to fit the punishment to the crime...later each part of the body given a value in weight of silver...mine is in gold. So…if someone was injured in a fight and lost a limb…the choice of money upfront or lose a limb option was available

If the option was trial by terror...an accused person was thrown into the river...if he survived…he was innocent and the accuser was put to death...my advice to the Sumerians take your children for early swimming lessons...it might save their life in adulthood
(Source:dk publishing the law)

The ten commandments
These were given to Moses and the land of Canaan...Moses led the Israelites to the promised land today called Palestine with people already on it. The evidence suggests that Moses does not exist outside of the Torah…as for the exodus and the promised land…according Historian Shlomo Sands never happened.

The Bible or Torah has multiple authors updated and revised over many years...reflecting the changing political and economic landscape…the five books of the Torah...are Genesis...Exodus…Leviticus…Numbers...Deuteronomy...today this means land theft and murder in Palestine…only the devout read these ancient texts today

Here are the Ten commandments
1)You shall worship no other god(goddess) before me...today means you will worship the ground your partner walks on

2)You shall not make an idol and worship...that means you should not be self-loving person...does not apply to me…I worship myself every day

3)Remember sabbath keep it holy... today means forget the sabbath and go play golf or some other activities

7

4)Honour you mother and father...only if they are prepared to pay for your wedding and deposit a for a house

5)You shall not murder...but you can murder a pizza or burger when you are really hungry

6)You shall not commit adultery...apply this today and half of the house of Commons will be empty...and most likely the place you work at

7)You shall not steal...unless you are the government...by stealth taxes

8)You shall not give false testimony against your neighbour...unless you have a dispute with them ...then...lie...lie...lie

9)You shall not covet anything that belongs to your neighbour...unless your neighbour's wife is super fit...you definitely want to covet her

10)Do not worship any other God...as God does not like competition

These absurd laws are now out of date and useless. Applying religious laws today leads to execution for adultery in Iran...cutting of hands for stealing...murder of medical staff at abortion clinics...land theft and murder in Palestine and other equally barbaric practices in other parts of the world in the name of religion...including circumcision...for boys and girls

You have prohibitions on pork and alcohol...ritualized slaughter of animals and other ridiculous practices...such as in Leviticus...to purify a house the priest takes some wood...yarn...live bird...dip in blood of a sacrificed bird plus water and sprinkle the house seven times

Then the bird would released...all the sins and house is now purified...this ritual could be an instant money maker today...accept sacrificing a live bird may upset the animal protection society

If the farmers bull was to gore someone and they died...the bull is to be stoned to death...and the owner put to death...however your life can be saved if you make a 'substantial cash offer'...today we have compensation for lost limbs...for victims of crime.

To summarise Jewish laws based on Moses...called Mosaic laws...written on scrolls with a quill...no mistakes allowed...the scrolls held in a flashy cabinet...in the holiest part of the synagogue...and to be forgotten and ignored in the real world

Today Mosaic laws used as justification for land theft and murder in Palestine...for religious ceremonies by the devout...and as a form of entertainment by less religious...mostly younger Jews
(Source:dk publishing the law)

China and heavenly delights
The King Zhou got rid of the Shang dynasty which had ruled China for 500 years. To justify the conquest, he used the 'mandate from heaven excuse'...he said the previous lot had neglected their 'heavenly duties'...so the mandate had been transferred to him

The Shang Kings also got their authority by communicating with ancestors...by analysing cracks in bones and turtle shells...today we call this 'lying with statistics'...Kings to rule justly or they will lose their mandates...today politicians lose their mandate by being voted out of office

Maritime laws...of the seas
Maritime laws invented by the Greeks and Romans to protect the stolen wealth from other regions they controlled...conquered...invaded or looted. The Greek Island of Rhodes was a hot spot for all the looted wealth

Today some of these maritime laws still exist...the law of jettison...if a ship has to dump stuff to prevent it from sinking...the losses to be shared...today we have the insurer Lloyd's of London who insure losses

How to rule well and not lose your head

Confucianism is based on the belief that traditions and family values are best for governing society...the five key relationships are:

1)Ruler to the ruled...the peasant class

2)Father to son...with China's low birth rate...a little difficult

3)Husband to wife...the important one ...she who must be obeyed

4)Older brother to younger brother…difficult with the low birth rate in China's one child policy

5)Friend to friend ...until you fall out with each other

In each of these relationships the dominant partner is the caring one. By setting good examples there should not be need for many laws...as society would be virtuous.

Daoism
Lead a simple life and get rid of greed and selfishness. Protection of private property sacrosanct…rulers must protect people's privacy...make no unjust laws and impose no restrictions. Today in the West this philosophy is called Libertarianism...limited role of government...freedom of the individual…yet to be put in practice

Legalism
Based on the assumption that people are lazy…feckless and useless...not far from the truth...so strong laws needed to deter crime and harsh punishment

Legalism was adopted in the 4th century in China by Shang Yang with terrible consequences...with mutilation...public executions...people boiled...collective punishment...or buried alive.

Under this brutal harsh system of fear and intimidation...a powerful unitary state was created and got rid of feudalism. However…when Shang fell from power he was subjected to the same laws and was ripped apart by chariots...his family were also killed ...the end of his blood line…in blood

Ruling by fear... peace and order was established...standard currency...weights and measures...simple writing introduced. The harsh rule however did not last... a less harsh regime emerged...still autocratic.

(Source:dk publishing the law)

Plato's laws

City states with an authoritarian system...with a little democracy. A dictator rules with a wise council and elected officials...who ensure no one is more powerful than the laws...i.e. With checks and balances.

Aristotle's laws

For Aristotle there is natural law and conventional law (man-made)
Natural laws are universal ...while conventional laws change. The debate between natural laws and conventional laws has been a constant battle which are important...and have not been resolved...prepare for more endless debates that get nowhere.

Stoicism...we are equal in front of God...on earth we are not so equal

The idea is natural law from heaven combined with reason leads to the good life...we are all equal and will live happily together. Trying to put this principle in the real world has been difficult.

In the real world there are classes of people and inequality between people in wealth and income...to have equal society you need fairly equal income distribution...difficult when small number of people end up with a large share of the income

Using 'God' as the final law giver...means many interpretations of the law and disagreements

Damage my property and you will pay
The Romans were the first to come with compensation for damage...if live stock or slaves (both the same thing) unlawfully

killed...market price to be paid...to be assessed in 30 days...insurance companies please note

India and the caste system
Two Hindu scripts have laid the caste system of India and poverty and inequality in society has become solidified. Indian society is divided into four classes:

Brahmins...Royalty class...get to have sex...for free...with the lower classes

The ruling class (Kshatriyas)...they ruled until the British arrived...who ruled over them

Vaishyas...farmers and merchants who actually created wealth for the upper classes to steal

Shudras...the peasant class or workers...you definitely do not want to belong to this class...with no upward mobility...you were doomed

You cannot marry in to another caste...or move to another caste ...the system is not as rigid as in the past ...with urbanization...caste still does have significant influence on Indian society.

Virtue and Justice...Utopian dream
The Roman Ulpian was the first person to define the concept of the good life...honesty...harm no one...each person gets what they deserve...all these sound very reasonable... impossible to put in practice

For him law should be about goodness and fairness...difficult to define...however the Romans managed to have a working legal system called Codex...which became the basis of civil law...widely used today...and circumvented by smart lawyers.

Truth...justice and peace
Let's murder the Jews European style
King of Persia lets the Jews return and build their Temple...as long as he got his share

The Jews under Roman rule had enough… revolted...the Romans destroy the temple to rubble...something the Palestinians in Gaza are familiar with

French Rabbi Yitzaki writes the Talmud...and is rewarded by the French state a life time supply of Baguettes and coffee

He gets done for Blasphemy...all copies of his book burned...to keep the French warm ...it was a cold winter…and no Baguettes or Coffee for the Rabbi

Bloomberg ...started later to publish the Talmud...today Bloomberg is a huge media giant...you get financial news from… and Talmud sermons… Bloomberg is also a big supporter of Israel

During Roman rule Temple worship...two rival forms of worship existed (1) aristocratic priests...only practised written laws (2) the other believed in oral tradition...at the end time...God would resurrect the dead...punish the wicked...reward the just...we need God to do this now...i come under the reward the 'just'category

The Romans trashed the Temple...leaving the Jews with a huge problem...no temple to worship…the Rabbi's managed to convince the Romans (shekels in their off shore bank accounts) to worship without a temple...prayer and study became the norm...that's probably why the Jews are so smart...and good at murdering Arabs.

Hadrian expelled the Jews...so the Rabbi's relied on a code of laws...how to be a good Jew...and how to be a bad Jew to your Arab neighbours. In the past the Jews found safe haven in Muslim lands...free from persecution...a favour which they have failed to return to the Palestinians. Jewish laws have taken much from Muslim laws...both sets of laws derived by scholarship and inquiry
(Source:dk publishing the law)

A walk on the wild side
Jesus Christ (not his real name) was nailed to a plank by the Romans for failing to file his tax return. His real name for Moshe

Cohen...he was the only son of Mary and his carpenter Dad...it was expected being Jewish he would follow the family tradition of making furniture

He however decided Philosophy was his passion...this deeply distressed his parents. At an early age he decided to have heated arguments with the Elders of his community about corrupt practices. He took affirmative action in the Temple turning over the tables of the money lenders...Goldman Sachs has been around a long time

This made him many enemies. They managed to pay someone to accuse and testify against him for criminal activities...he was accused of the following:

1)Failure to file tax return

2)illicit relationships...no witnesses were called

3)Drunk and disorderly while riding his donkey…he was banned for three months and three points put on his licence

4)Cooking and cleaning on Saturday...the day of rest for the Jewish community

5)Terrorising the neighbourhood with his gang of 12 followers

6)Failure to register his business 'fishes and loaves' and declare earnings and pay the sales tax due

7)Making wine without a 'Liquor' licence...selling alcohol to under 18 years old

8)Practising medicine...without a medical licence...making the 'blind see'

With all the above accusations it was going to be very difficult to deny all charge…. the jury found him guilty...however he did create a new Religion...and Roman Catholic law...known as Canon law. After his death his followers carried on with his good works...rituals of communion of holy bread and wine...lots of wine

New converts were Baptized…many were more interested in the 'bread and wine'.As the religion spread and the 'wine' flowed the Bishops and Churches became important

Christianity…unique selling point it offered salvation to sinners...to go on to commit more sins...and damnation of hell fire and torture for the baddies. In Europe the Church became the state for 300 years…known as the 'dark ages' nothing much changed…no material or social progress for ordinary people

The Church would inflict terrible punishment for blasphemy and other minor offences. Reading the Bible was compulsory...other religions frowned upon or banned in public

As Christianity became popular with the 'one God' hypothesis...the Romans with their many Gods were concerned. They passed a law that all must make sacrifices to the Roman Gods or face the death penalty

The bishops began not only make people obey God's laws but also make their own laws. The Roman emperor Constantine who became a Christian convert...gave Christian's freedom to worship without persecution

Something the Jews in Israel need to learn at the Al Aqsa Mosque. He also gave them Back their own stolen property…he was an all-round nice emperor

Constantine gave the bishops legitimacy backed by state power. However… there were splits in the Church... arguments about God...the holy Ghost and the Son...who was more important.

It was decided God is number 1…the son number 2… and the holy Ghost number 3. Constantine organised a council of Bishops...the council decided the various religious holidays...what to teach…what to do with the pagans

The Christian emperor Theodosius passed a law for everyone to become a Christian...if you refused you were considered 'demented and insane'...this was a great way to make Christians and fill up the 'Lunatic asylum'

The effect of Canon law was that everyone goes to Church...fasting and reading the bible and prayers. Today with the decline of Christianity...the only thing many people practice is 'fasting' as a way to lose weight. The Western world is unique in that Church laws are the basis of the present legal system

In Islam in the 7th century the Prophet Muhammad (peace be upon him) emerged in the Middle East… he unified the various tribes under the new Religion of Islam. The legal system is based on the Koranic text...the Hadiths verified by Islamic Scholars...which are the basis of sharia law...which is civil law under Islam...much misunderstood in the West

Meanwhile in little old England the Norman King William created a new feudal system of land tenure. His book the Doomsday book is the first inventory of land and property in the UK...this would be used later to make property law cases

In 12th century a new innovation of travelling justices in assize courts would hear cases in towns and cities and dispense justice...common law for the common people

The Magna Carta was the first document which gave ordinary citizens protection under the law from arbitrary arrest and detention and access to the law...both Canon law and civil law existed side by side...later the merchants were responsible for creating commercial laws to regulate trade

Trial by torture
This type of justice was very popular in the Middle Ages

The accused had to take a stone from boiling water...depth of water dependent on the severity of the crime…. after three days the hand unwrapped of its bandage …if it healed you were innocent

People made to walk on hot coal…if blisters healed...innocent...this should be used on our forever lying

Politicians...being unable to walk for a few days may make them more honest

Both accused and defendant made to stand with arms outstretched...the first one to drop their arm lost the case...this is a great way to resolve cases...it is non- violent ...no injuries sustained...and people can train for the event...to give them a better chance of winning

Trial by combat...duels were popular among the upper classes...often professional 'hit men' were hired...the rules were strictly enforced by a judge...the winner was the one... who did not sustain more physical harm than the other person...serious injuries even death was the outcome. The loser would lose his property and other losses

Trial by torture occurred if in a case there were no witnesses or evidence...the rich landowners used it to settle land disputes...while the poor would be fined

Islamic law
The Prophet Muhammad (peace be upon him) emerged as a very important figure in the 7th century...at this time there were many warring tribes...worship of many Gods and paganism

The Prophet (peace be upon him) received God's revelations which became the Koran. After receiving the word of God he preached the oneness of God as revealed to him. However other tribes resented his preachings and on a number of occasions he barely escaped with his life...many attempts were made on his life

He managed to create enough followers in what we now call the umma...he was able to defeat his enemies. The word of the Koran spread to the whole of the Middle East and Islam spread to many parts of the world

The basis of the Koran are very simple...pray five times a day...be charitable to the poor...pay the Zakat...what we now call wealth tax...at the end of your life to visit the Holiest city of Islam... Mecca...what is known as Haj

This is the time you must be honest with yourself and time for reflection...ask God for forgiveness...cleanse your soul and prepare yourself for your day of judgement when God will decide your fate

The Koran is the source of all Islamic law

The Hadiths...are the sayings and the actions of the Prophet (peace be upon him)

If the Koran and Hadiths are unable to answer a particular legal problem...Judges may decide how the Koran and Hadith would deal with this in a similar way

Independent logical reasoning by judges is allowed as long as the public welfare benefits

Judges may also consult Islamic scholars for guidance in making rulings

Source of Islamic law
As Islam spread a consistent legal framework became necessary...Islamic civil law grew...Islamic judges...and Islamic legal Scholars called Muftis ...who could be consulted on matters of religious laws and issue Fatwas

The Sunna...a body of legal and social practices...were a guide how to be a good and pious Muslim

The Hanifa is the oldest of the Islamic civil laws...Al-Bukhari compiled and collected the most important and authentic Hadiths. It was decided that the Koran and Hadiths must be made consistent with each other...reasoning and consideration for the welfare of the Islamic community is prime consideration...in making legal decisions

Formal legal schools were established ...such as the Hanfi...Maliki...Shafi and Hanbali. There was split in Islam with now Shia and Sunni divide... which led to different interpretations of Islamic law

Law and order in the Islamic world
Islamic law works on a number of principles (1) compulsory (2) recommended (3) neutral (4) reprehensible (5) forbidden...serious crime like murder and rape carried severe punishments...but the evidence needed was much higher

Because lack of witnesses to crimes...much of criminal law transferred to state courts under the Abbasids dynasty. The Ottomans went much further in creating civil laws not necessarily based on Islamic law...this has created tensions even today...how far does Islamic law and common law go

Sharia law today based on the Koran and Hadiths operates in many Muslim countries with varying degrees. The Taliban in Afghanistan only Sharia law is used. Other Muslim countries have tried to reconcile Sharia law with the conventional legal system either inherited from the colonial era or has existed before Islam or during Islamic history
(Source:dk publishing the law)

Buy land God is not making it any more
Bad boy William of Normandy invaded and took the land of the Aristocracy in England...he keeps around 17% and gives the rest to feudal barons as long as they served his interests.

The Domesday book compiles all land in England and their values...so we can say that bad boy William was the first Estate agent in England...and he could provide title deeds to land and property rights.

To this day the Domesday book is the foundation of the British legal system and its problems...a legal system over 800 years old and out of date...leading to many property disputes and other issues.

In the UK you may own your home but not the land...on which you pay small rent called ground rent. Sometime a go a person bought or took ownership of a strip land in front of a row of houses. He then sent letters informing the house owners every time they left their house...they would be trespassing on his land.

He therefore was entitled to charge them for the use of his land or stop them...he sent each of them a bill for $2000.The owners complained they have no choice as they need to cross his land to access the public highways and footpaths.

The issue ended up in the courts and the landowner won...because in law he was right...The local council and local Politicians had to come up with a solution...they managed to reduce the amount but could not overturn the old...out of date law.

Gratian Law
The issue of how to reconcile Roman laws with Church laws. A person called Gratian made a good attempt at this...here is his solution:

1)A consistent framework of Roman and civil law needed

2)He revised Canon law to include the following: -

3)Property rights...no one should take without due process of law

4)Freedom to choose...who you want to marry

5)Cannot be tried twice for the same crime

Donald Trump...the ridiculous cases brought against him...without any merit or evidence...this is known as law fare...the idea to entangle the person in endless legal cases

Gratian was able to create an alternative legal framework to the Church while encompassing many aspects of Church Canon laws...end result society is better off and the Church not so happy to lose so much influence

Fat slob Henry1I1 who hated the Catholic Church got fed up with sending them gold and silver every year...he decided to reform the legal system without Church influence...his solution as follows:
1)Travelling Judges tour the country

2)Juries made of 'free' people not tied to land or owned by land Barons

3)Judges determine trial by torture...the water treatment

4)Guilty lose property and a foot...others can be exiled

Many of the accused fled before the court proceedings...and with good reason...but they lost their property...so each accused had to make decision ...lose a foot or lose a house...this is tough call
Things improved later with jury of 12 which we have today
(Source:dk publishing the law)

The Monarch extortion racket
Under bad boy King William...he set up a system where Barons given land and peasants to exploit... paid allegiance and dues to the King.However...with all the wars the Monarchs were involved in... the Monarch needed more and more money from the Barons...who became very resentful

Monarch set up Royal courts to reduce Baron powers....war with France led to financial problems for Monarch...solution don't go to war with France

Barons revolt...Magna Carta...Monarch forced to sign... the Monarchs power reduced...not arresting of people without evidence or due process of law passed

The Magna Carta was a document to protect the Barons...not the people ...it later became the people's charter...when an independent judiciary emerged

Later royals tried to reduce or get rid of the charter with limited success...as parliament was formed as counter to Royal decrees

In essence the power shifted from the Royals to the Barons to Parliament

Today many of the provisions of the Magna Carta no longer exist...but it still remains the basis of the British Legal system

Common Good
The issue of how laws come about and whether universal or not.
Thomas Aquinas was one of the first to deal with this issue:

1)People have the ability to reason (very limited) and live in harmony (not very often)

2)Heavenly laws embedded in nature…unless you are a non-believer

3)Heavenly laws better than man-made laws...do not change (and do not work)

4)Heavenly and universal laws good for society… two wrongs do not make a right

5)I cannot believe anybody believes this nonsense today...laws are made by the powerful in society to protect their interests not yours

6)Nice try Aquinas...you get a d- for this essay...must try harder next time

The concept of natural law emerging… eternal laws emerging from heavenly laws ...is a non-starter in the real world. Anyone living in the US knows minor infringements of the law can lead to terrible consequences...a person in the US was given a long prison sentence for stealing a pizza ...which natural or heavenly law used to convict her

Laws are either just or unjust...the collective West has imposed Universal laws through wars...Colonialism and imperialism...no natural laws...or heavenly laws...or universal laws...or just laws...only laws to protect the rights and interests of the rich and powerful countries.

Commercial laws…how to steal legally
Early on merchants developed their private laws to settle disputes and regulate trade dealings...especially maritime laws. Merchants from the countries doing business agreed to a set of rules applicable to all...these in essence 'codes of conduct'. The Italian cities of Genoa and Venice were at the fore front of maritime laws…66 articles.

Piracy was a big problem… a trading organization developed around the region encompassing ports and cities to give protection to Merchants.In Little Old England royal decree gave freedom of navigation to foreign merchants and speedy justice

Interesting to note much of wealth by merchants was stolen from colonies under an Empire system...so piracy protection was to stop the stolen wealth from being stolen again

Merchant's courts
Special merchant's courts administered and settled disputes...this led to bills of laden (promissory notes) …which could act as money or settlement of transactions...with the knowledge in case off dispute the Merchant courts could act.
Merchant courts fell into disrepute...as they were voluntary...laws were different depending which country you use...which applied laws differently...so a dispute settled in London would not be accepted in Italy. They were eventually replaced by National laws of the lands. International maritime laws still exist to manage piracy…and private disputes that do not involve states

However no international laws maritime or otherwise applies to the US...stealing Syrian oil and selling it on the open market is normal business practice for the US.

Empire…Enlightenment and exploitation
Venice emerged as a major trading power...made its own maritime laws. The rise of Empires the world divided among them...international order...the peace of Westphalia… let's stop killing each other in Europe...instead conquer the rest of the world and exploit.

New international laws to justify land theft…murder…slaves…exploitation of resources and people...and enlightenment

Reason over faith...progress and liberty and tolerance unless you were a colonial subject or slave...none of the above applied

Bill of rights in the UK...not for slaves or colonial subjects

The US independence.1776...constitution life...liberty...and pursuit of happiness...but not for slaves

Government by the people for the people...today in the US means...government by corporate interests for the corporate interests

Patent laws...you steal from me...i steal from you
The idea of a patent is to give the holder temporary protection for a short period of time recoup his time and money spent. The Italians were the first to get into the patent acts and registration of patents.

They established patent registration...rules for use and time period and transfer of patents. A patent had to be unique not obvious...with ten years of patent protection...and no copying...fines imposed. These laws made Venice the Tech hub of Europe for innovation.

As the number of patents increase so did the number of patent lawyers. As patents at this time were national...in little old England they added to patent rules to grant monopolies to sell patented products.

The effect of granting patent monopoly was to deter not encourage innovation. The 'coke'laws got rid of monopoly rights...patents can only be granted for new or original ideas

In the real world today there two types of patents...product patent and process patent. Product patent is new... while a process patent is where you can make something better or cheaper for a new or existing patent.

In practice this is how it works
Imagine you are a car manufacturer and you make a car using your own patents...from body...to engine to tyres...Now imagine the tyres have a pattern on which the US has a patent. They can

decide who you can sell the vehicle to ...disobey the Master and sanctions are coming your way

Now imagine a product like a pain killer... aspirin...the patent on which has expired...imagine your company has devised a process where you can make it cheaper and in more quantities.

You can be blocked because the original patent holder can prevent you making Aspirin cheaper. It gets worst a Japanese tried to patent the production and use of 'Haldi' a common ingredient in Indian cooking. Had he succeeded he would work out how much 'haldi'used in India and extort the money from the Indian government. Fortunately...this person was stopped when the Indian government contested the claim in court.

Today with free stuff online and people giving the use of ideas and inventions for free and relying on voluntary donations...the old patent system is not working well. Patents are used today to stop innovation...which can harm the economic prospects of an existing patent or new patent.

China is now the greatest issuer of new patents...basically existing patents...altered or modified to make them new. A patent is only good if you have the money to protect it...most inventors do not have the money for protection ...so patent theft is rife...with converging technology it is difficult to come up with something new or original.

The only boom in the patent industry is the number off patent lawyers...my advice become a patent lawyer...you will make more money than from owning a patent

The treaty of Colonialism
In 387ce treaty divide the Persian and Byzantine empire

1750 treaty Spain and Portugal divide their empire

1885 Berlin conference...Africa divided among the European Empires

Columbus discovers the New World already discovered by the people living there...claimed it for Spain...land theft and murder follows

Portugal disputed his claims...the Pope was asked to settle the dispute...he divided the world in two...Portugal moved the lines and got more territory...a treaty was signed to avoid a war

For local inhabitants it was bad news ...they got wiped out...disease...land theft...murder and rape...estimates vary... more than 15 million perished

Portugal got Brazil and they speak Portuguese now...while the rest of Latin America became Spanish and speak Spanish

Making poverty pay
The modern welfare state is a German idea...they were the first to implement it
Poor laws were introduced in little Old England ...to help the poor stay poor

Too many beggars and down and outs were a nuisance...contributing to anti-social behaviour and criminality...the House of Lords is full of them...ex-members of parliament and retired do goodies

Charity only makes people lazy...when they should be working...taxes should be used to help the poor...get them off the streets...better for society

The poor should be encouraged to work...by being exploited and used as cheap labour
In the real world the 'black death' killed 30-40% of Europe's population...this created a labour shortage and a rise in wages. In order to stop them moving to higher wage areas...laws passed to keep them from being mobile...so that they could be used as cheap labour. If they moved out of their area...they were caught and whipped.

People were forced to take low paid and unpleasant jobs...others who refused to work sent to 'correction camps' to be 'educated'. The economic circumstances at the time were...grain prices rose sharply...wages declined by 60%...hospitals and charities were ended...bad news if you were poor

Fat slob Henry the V111 smashed the churches ...the poor relied on them for charity. Poor laws introduced to provide a basic safety net...taxes introduced to pay for welfare...parents and children must look after each other...the idea helping the poor is good for society

The deserving poor versus the non-deserving
As the number of poor has increased so has the resentment against and what to do with them. The poor were classified as living indoor or outdoor. The indoor were given money called 'dole'...a term still used today to refer to welfare.

The indoor also made to work as cheap labour. The Outdoor dragged and put to work ...in 'workhouses'...in harsh conditions...to deter them from becoming welfare dependent. The anti-social were sent to 'correction facilities'...harsher conditions and harder labour.

Bridwell prison was one such correction facility...harsh conditions and hard labour ...with regular whippings... for inmates twice a week... was the only entertainment.

A fierce debate took place where people like the 'economist 'Ricardo' said poor relief undermined the work ethic...this debate led to a new poor law in 1834...workhouses with even harsher...inhumane conditions. The Victorian 'sweat shops' remained for 100 years before being abolished in 1948

In the real world the conditions mentioned above still exist today in sweat shops all over the world...the capitalists still exploits cheap labour ..men...women...and children in third world countries...which is very humane of the rich countries to export 'slave work conditions' in the name of bringing jobs and prosperity to these countries

War and Peace
Grotius the original founder of international laws. He believed universal laws applied to states and disputes should be settled by dialogue and not resort to war. War should only be used in extreme circumstances to defend one's country or its interests and force used must be proportionate…i.e. just war theory.

In the real-world powerful countries like the US use international law when it suits them and ignore it when it does not. Fake evidence used to invade Iraq…along with that nasty little country 'little old England' who is up the rear end of the Americans…ready to do America's dirty work…anywhere in the world

The genocide that is being committed by Israel against a helpless...defenceless population of Gaza are war crimes...yet no one is willing to do anything...in fact Western countries are queuing up to Israel to encourage it and support it militarily...economically and diplomatically to carry on the genocide...why ? Here is my reason

International law if applied selectively becomes meaningless...if powerful rich countries can ignore it at their will...what is the purpose of international law. It appears the world is reverting back to 19th century gun boat diplomacy...might is right as power shifts from the West to the East prepare for more conflicts

The lunatics that run the Pentagon believe they can win a nuclear war ...there is an old saying 'the lunatics have taken over the Asylum'. The US has to decide…to let the rest of the world get along without it… or it wants full spectrum dominance...…. the coming election will decide this

The Peace of Westphalia
After hundreds of years of Europeans killing themselves in endless wars...they decided to try peace. The treaty of Westphalia

recognized states...sovereignty and boundaries. It came about...
after the thirty years war...the Hapsburg empire versus the
Bourbon of France...Sweden and Spain...these conflicts were very
damaging...Bourbon today is a very nice biscuit and a popular
Whisky

**In the real world ...Westphalia treaty is the basis of
international order**...the so called 'rule-based order'...but who
made the rules...was it a democratic process...the UN and its
charter represents the interests of the old Colonial and Imperial
powers...the UN security council being the classic example

The only time the UN is democratic is in the national assembly
vote where all countries get to vote...yet its decision is not
binding...what a joke...the UN should be made democratic or
abandoned...it's not fit for purpose.

The trial of King Charles 1
The Monarchy... right to rule was based on the Devine right of
Kings...from God. This issue came to a head in three civil wars
which led to parliament being sovereign and not the King. Charlie
boy was tried ad executed. The present King Charles must be
made aware of what happened to his past relative if he gets out of
line
The Monarchy came back with vengeance with Charles 11...who
executed the people who executed his relative Charles 1. In the
real world the Monarch is very wealthy...the Crown estate
manages the Kings assets...mostly land and property in trust on
behalf of the Crown
If the UK was to get rid of the Monarchy there would be a legal
and constitutional crisis. The state would have to compensate the
Crown for seizing its assets...which could be $billions of dollars

Slave colonies
Slavery which we now regard as inhumane was quite common
in the past. You were either a slave or subject under an empire
system...even the Bible endorses slavery...however the Europeans
and the US industrialized the process by transporting millions for
plantations.

When the US declared independence in 1776 there were already 500,000 slaves. The Dutch...Portuguese and British also got into the slave owning business. In the US cotton plantations used most slaves...in other countries sugar plantations.

Laws were passed which made the slaves and their children property of the slave master or plantation…these slave codes gave total control over the slaves as goods to be traded or abused…i.e. chattel slavery.

Slaves could be punished for the most minor offences with whippings ..branding...prison...even if a slave died due to severe punishment the Slave master had immunity from prosecution.

Slaves were not taught to read and write. The main fear of Slave masters was slave rebellions as their numbers grew. The Slave Nat Turner led a slave rebellion killing over 50 white people...before being caught and executed with others

As for slave women they worked all day on the plantations and in the evening they 'served 'their white colonial master ...every kind of sexual degradation practiced on these poor unfortunate 'souls'.The children from these encounters (sex abuse/rape) were also slaves

Girls as young as 13 years impregnated so they could produce more slave children...there were 15 slave states in the US. Although slavery ended in 1865...the slave mind set did not end till much later. It was only after the civil rights movements in the1960's that Blacks in America got full citizenship rights and Alabama only made mixed relationships legal in 2000

In the real world the effects of slavery are still with us today. The Black Diaspora around the world is due to past slavery. Sadly… to be black in most parts of the world means to be poor and often marginalized. I am in Pakistan as I am writing this.

The Islamic empire practised slavery for over 1000 years. Today the descendants of these slaves are citizens of these countries. In Pakistan the 'darker' skinned Pakistani's are among the poorest in this country...you find many in the Sind region of Pakistan…the poorest region with the richest landlords. They are tolerated but not liked...from some of the comments I have read on social media...polite things are not said about them

Hopefully over time attitudes may change...the best I can hope for is they are tolerated but not discriminated. In other parts of the world the story is similar...the 'darker you are...the poorer you are'

The Bill of rights...the bill for nobody
This document arose due to the conflict between Protestants and Catholics when King James gave both religions equal rights to worship and protest. This did not end well as he was deposed replaced by William of Orange. Parliament offered the crown to others who signed a bill of rights...passing power from Crown to Parliament to the people

1)Gave tax raising powers...and people certainly are taxed today

2)Freedom of speech...say something contentious and you will be prosecuted

3)Raising of army...for the endless wars the UK is involved in…and being up the 'rear end of the Americans'

The bill of rights is the bill for nobody as it never has done...or will do...protect peoples fundamental rights. Recently a Palestinian Doctor was arrested by Police in the UK...no valid reason given...most likely his anti-Israel comments got him into trouble...his arrest and release ...was a warning to others...keep quite or we will arrest you

A former Politician who criticized Israel's Gaza genocide was arrested after 'false 'allegations about a rape.... acts like this make the UK worse than a Banana Republic...so people in the UK need to be aware they have no rights ...only on paper...not in reality

Salem witch trials...hysteria gone mad

A local Ministers Daughter started to act strangely...since at that time no Psychologists around to make an assessment...it was assumed it was the work of the devil. She accused three local girls of witchcraft...the women confessed hoping to save themselves

The resulting mass hysteria led to the death of 19 people...mostly women...no actual evidence was produced. Things became so bad that a local Governors wife was accused of witchcraft. He changed the rules by not allowing hearsay evidence and set up new courts with much tougher levels of evidence required. This saved his wife and further accusations being made...and the lives of others

Some 200 people were accused of Witchcraft...besides making the Town a laughing stock...it must have been very entertaining...before Television and mass media. One poor person accused refused to admit his guilt ...a plank was placed on his body and heavy stones placed on the plank until he stopped breathing...he died two days later...no confession however...he died an innocent man.

What this episode in American history tells us... if you mix religion with mental health issues...hysteria can develop and lead to terrible consequences...today however accusations without evidence are the least credible evidence...and the accusers above...today would be locked in prison or a mental health institute today

Books and copy rights
When the German Guttenberg invented the printing press...it changed the world forever and created problems of copying and how to stop or control it. In England the Caxton press was used to print books.

Authors realized if their work could be copied...they would lose money. A law was passed to give one company called the Stationers company sole rights to publish books...the author received a small royalty.

However...critics of this arrangement argued that was against the national interest giving exclusive rights to one company...the copyright law was passed ...which gave copyright protection for only a number of years. The authors were put in charge and decide who is allowed to publish their works. Also... a number of copied books put in designated 'libraries'

In the real world copying of books is rife...the photocopier has made it easier...The rise of digital print media is the death sentence for the book printing industry. Retailers like Amazon allow authors to bypass the traditional book printers and sell directly to the public in digital format and there is pdf...free books. My works are only available on Amazon

When this book is published it will be digital first and if sales go well the printed version will be available...this is the future of book publishing...there are now digital libraries as past printed books are being digitized.

International law...to be ignored by the powerful Diplomat Vattel was the first person to put in writing the concept of international laws...how states govern relations with each other...now known as statecraft. He argued states like people should be free and independent...and free from foreign interference...the US and EU please take note

His main concern was that free trade between nations can only be secured by international recognition by all states to their duties and obligations to other states. The American Colonialists who were fighting- tax wars -with the British at that time used his argument to avoid paying taxes and secure independence.

In the real-world states like the US and EU interfere in the affairs of other countries all the time...no respect for the rules based international order. The US has invaded over 50 countries...killed over 20 million people...caused $billions of damages...stealing of resources of other countries...and there is no stopping the worlds military superpower...the Pentagon gone mad.

Common law...but not for the common people

William Blackstone was the first to publish a set of common laws...accessible for people to use and abuse. It gave clear explanations of complex legal cases. This text of common law was applied unevenly against the common people. If you were poor and uneducated the legal system was not your 'best friend'

The impact of this book has been wide...the new independent US used it as a legal foundational text...and used in the common wealth. The books emphasis is that people's property and their rights must be protected...very idealistic ...does not apply in the real world...welcome to the UK'S hate laws where anyone can make an allegation of being 'hurt' by a social media comment verbal or written and the Police will turn up at your house to arrest you ...end of free speech

The US political system

After independence the colonies were granted independence status. However, this created the problem of a unified tax system and a national defence force. The colonies main concern was the centralization of power leading to the same situation as with the British.

The solution… create two elected chambers to act as checks and balances against abuse of power. The electoral college elects the President. As a result of US history… and not to repeat their interactions with their former master little old England they have created a system which does not work

You have Congress...the Senate...a federal...state and local system...the supreme court...Federal courts...and the President...the bill of rights. With such a cumbersome political system...the beneficiaries are the increasing numbers of lawyers needed to manage the system.

The bill of rights...the most famous line...all men are equal…life…liberty and pursuit of happiness... (excludes women and slaves...they would have to wait a little longer).

Also in Abraham Lincoln's speech...Government of the people ...by the people...for the people. Translated today ...the government by the corporate interests...for the corporate interests.

In the real world the US political process is bought and paid for by corporate interests with elections now running into $billions of dollars...the whole system is corrupt to the core...the average voter has no influence on the Political process. Countless studies show that what the people want and what the Political process delivers is not the same

An MIT Social scientist has come up with the concept of 'investment theory of politics'...every election time corporate interests coalesce around a particular party that will best represent their interests.

Today both parties are pro-business...this is reflected in the business-friendly legislation being passed. The role of President is now more ceremonial...Barack Obama the first Black President and the most useless...was not able to pass universal health care legislation...blocked by Congress.

The checks and balances designed originally are now used to block legislation...the Congress being the main 'blocker'. However...Presidents still have the means to wage endless wars around the world to keep the arms industry profitable...America spends close to $1 trillion dollars on defence...tax payers' money funding the Arms industry while their infrastructure collapses.

The rights of man (and women a lot later)
After the French revolution a charter emerged giving most citizens equal rights. The history that gave rise to the French revolution is an interesting one. The Monarch needed money for all the wars the country was involved in. The wealthy who lent him the money wanted it back with interest...lots of interest

The only way was to tax the French subjects...most were poverty stricken. When they could no longer afford their favourite breakfast 'croissant and coffee' they rioted...the queen famously said ...if you cannot afford 'croissant and coffee…let them eat cake instead. This made the subjects even angrier and she lost her head...along with other Royalty and aristocracy…in future do not offer your subjects cake…can make them very angry

The French being very pragmatic people devised their own way of killing large number of people...the Guillotine...now in a museum...but still in working order if the need arises. The great French Philosophers Rousseau and Voltaire were asked for new charter of human rights they proposed

1)All men equal…no one has the right to rule over others

2)Men can choose who should govern them

3)Rule by consent only

4)Freedom to worship...free speech and freedom of the press

5)The Charter gave rights to men only...over 25 yrs. old with property…later it was changed to include others. Had the Monarch kept the price of flour low or not offered cake… it is unlikely there would have been a riot…and many heads would have been saved

Studies show that when a population spends more than 40% on basic needs... (enough to eat) ...they are more likely to riot. The Arab Spring uprising in Egypt was mainly due to rapid rise in price of flour. If there any Monarchs or Dictators out there...keep the price of flour low

After the French revolution things went worst not better...then Napoleon brought order but he went on the rampage all over Europe...decided he was the Emperor of Europe. Once industrialization came about the...standard of living for the French people rose rapidly...with Democracy and its Empire which it exploited.

(Source:dk publishing the law)

The rise of the 20th century

36

The rise of industrial capitalism in the early 20th century was transformative...it got rid of the feudal landlord class...freed people from the land to work in factories...as free labour...unions demanded better pay and conditions...the will of the people... in rise of Democracy as the best form of government.

The Europeans who have spent more than 1000 years killing each other had a war to end all wars the first world war...however the job was not done ...another war was needed to purge Europeans that dialogue not war... is the best way to settle disputes

With the change in society...a new legal framework was needed. The US constitution was amended to protect citizens from the abuse of power...the Supreme court to defend the people. In France a new civil code to protect citizens rights. In Little old England...worker rights...new Police force with nice blue uniforms...pointy hat and truncheons to beat people with introduced

Later on...consumers rights legislation to protect people from harmful or dangerous products. Women given the vote much later...in the US Jim crow laws segregation...it took the civil rights movements of the 1960's to get rid of this legislation.

Meanwhile in Germany the industrial powerhouse of Europe defeated twice. Hitler came to power...prime interest to overturn the Versailles treaty...the Jews in Germany became the 'enemy within'... his intention to deport them

In Russia Lenin came to power...equality for all...formation of workers coops...he died too early to fully implement the reforms...to be replaced by a Paranoid Psychopath called Stalin...death of over 25 million Russians ...no Democracy or human rights...until much later

The terrible history of death and destruction finally made Europeans think differently...that things must change...fortunately they have not learnt that lesson...they still interfere in the affairs of other countries...right now they are supporting Israel while it commits genocide in the 21st century… in real time… can be viewed on prime-time news media and internet…AL Jazeera is the best

The US Supreme Court…not so Supreme
The US Supreme court is the final check against abuse of government power...what is known as judicial review...so any legislation passed can be taken to court for a final verdict

In the real world the six Judges are appointed after a thorough selection process about their legal knowledge...social and political views...as well as their personal life under review…Once selected they are for life.

Recently Conservative pro-life judges have over turned a ruling which has now made abortion illegal. However…each state has to decide whether to abide by this ruling or not...it has caused a huge political storm...among women's groups who believe that they have the right to an abortion...as it's their body

Politicians are increasingly using the courts in the US to settle political disputes which are vote losers…in effect they are asking Judges to make 'political judgements'...the Judges have wisely thrown these cases out...on the grounds that they are political decisions to be made by politicians ...not legal decisions

The original US constitution has been gradually eroded...as politics weighs heavily on the Justice system. As an example…a law has been passed that gives corporations the same rights as a 'person'.
With business-friendly legislation... the justice system weighs heavily against the interest of ordinary citizens. So not only have the corporations bought up the electoral process...but the legal system is now up for sale. Justice and the law parted years ago….
RIP Justice in the US

The Napoleonic code

Despite all his faults Napoleon did get some things right which the French have benefited from. Prior to the revolution laws were made by the Church and the Barons and other powerful groups...there was a hotchpotch of laws and regulations.

What Napoleon did was to unify the legal system under the 'Napoleonic codes. These laws gave people basic rights...free from religious persecution...simplified civil and commercial laws...with less government interference. The Napoleonic laws would be used by other countries as a basic legal frame work to build on.

However... the laws did not prevent the relentless persecution of the poor and marginalized in society. Even today in the land of the free and brave...the US ...the laws are unevenly applied...the poor or least well off do not get the justice they deserve

The Slave trade ...profit at its best
Slavery has existed in the past in many civilizations in one form or another. By converting people into a commodity...you can treat them as you wish. It was the Europeans who turned slavery into an industry...the Democracy loving British the worst offenders

Much has been written about slavery...however what is not often mentioned is the economics of slavery. The reason it lasted so long was that it was profitable and the main reason for its abolition was it became unprofitable with the rise of industry and mechanized labour.

It is estimated around 10-12 million slaves exported with around 2.5 million dying on route. They were used in the colonies of the French...Dutch…Belgium...British and the US...on plantations to produce tobacco…sugar...molasses...rum...and cotton

The slave trade made many millionaires...read the book 'the sugar Barons'. In the UK investing in the 'slavery business' was normal...there were companies you could buy shares in… which traded in slaves...many ordinary British people saw it as a good investment… as a pension…or savings scheme

With the revolutions in America and France and equality for all ...the issue of slavery began to be discussed. The Abolitionists grew in number on both sides of the Atlantic...arguing you cannot have freedom for one group and ignore another...namely the slaves.

In the UK William Wilberforce was a leading reformist...spent 20 years bringing anti-slavery bills to parliament. At first many politicians were reluctant as they had a direct investment in the slave trade. A bill was eventually passed...but the slave owners had to be compensated for 'loss of property' from the public...yes the taxpayer once again conned.

In the land of the free and brave the US...the issue was… As the North non-slave owning group versus the South...the slave owners. Once again…the issue was economic…the North resented slavery because it competed with 'free labour'...i.e. it undercut the wages of the free locals in the US. This gave the South an unfair economic advantage in trade...created resentment in the North...and the other issue was the South wanted independence

The slavery excuse used as justification to start a war and keep the country unified. The Blacks in the South offered freedom if they fought with the Northern states. After the defeat of the South and laws passed to give the slaves rights...the biggest movement of people from the South to the North took place …mostly the freed black slaves in the US…moved from the South to the North of the country

The South however defeated… managed to turn slaves into bonded labour…debt peonage...which continued to enslave many blacks for generations...Jim crow laws and segregation persisted well in to the 1960's

Today estimates of up 45 million slaves world-wide…in the form of bonded labour exist...you can see this in India and

Pakistan...where debt is passed from one generation to the next...despite these countries having signed up to anti-slavery mandates in international law.

With the internet...mass media and social media...slavery practices... are being exposed...hopefully the 'worldwide moral community' ... and pressure will have some lasting influence in changing people's attitudes and get rid of this despicable practice of turning people into property

(Source:dk publishing the law)

Warning...**Slavery only ended when it was no longer economically viable**...and the money made from slavery kick started the Industrial revolution. You can pass laws...but changing people's attitudes is more difficult.

The Police ...or military force in another uniform
Every country has a Police force...in some countries they act to deter crime and bring criminals to justice...in other countries they are used as a para-military force to enforce law and order and deter dissent.

Warning...**the main purpose of the Police is law and order**...to prevent the population getting of control... as for crime...the rate of criminal convictions is very low

In the past policing was an ad hoc business...people would band together and form vigilante groups

In little old England...an act created justices of the peace...they administered local justice...assuming you could catch the criminals

The wealthy formed their own private 'army' whose job to get back stolen goods

The commercial heart of London created its own 'police force 'called the Bow Street runners'...working for the Bow Street magistrates...to issue summons and writs

41

More reforms and more laws...the first professional police force called the Thames River Police...they could swim and apprehend criminals...crime fell sharply

The Metropolitan police act created the modern police force...a new uniform...pointy hat...and a new truncheon to beat people with...the British Policing model has been adopted by other countries...with equally dismal results

Gambling...the stupidity tax

Gambling has been around a long time...in little old England people gambled on bear baiting...cockfighting...while the rich played dice or card games. Religion has always been against gambling...it can lead to financial ruin and less money for the church

States have decided to regulate and tax it. In the UK when you make a bet a %percentage goes to the tax man. Licensed gambling is now permitted in the UK...there are betting shops on every high street. Gambling now has gone online...taxing the 'poor' is now legal and legitimate

Whenever you gamble the odds are stacked against you...in a casino there is a built in %percentage that goes to the house and the tax man...now with the national lottery the state is the croupier...hence the stupidity tax...used to fund good causes.

Animal rights
Before cars and trucks animal power was used...horses...donkeys...etc as work animals. Animal cruelty was quite common. Animal cruelty acts passed...banned badger baiting...protection for cats and dogs. Today we have better understanding that animals do suffer and can be overworked

I am in Pakistan as I write this where animal labour is quite common...the good thing is that it is declining as more mechanical means of moving stuff is becoming available...my guess animal labour will be reduced by further 90% in the next ten years...as the country rapidly urbanises and industrializes.

Contract law...100% enforceable by the Mafia
Modern contract law is based on a single case in Little Old England in 1854. Hadley versus Baxendale. Hadley was a mill owner… a part of the equipment used to process the flour broke...they ordered a new one from Baxendale's...they sent the old one and expected a new one the next day...it did not arrive till seven days later

Hadley's suffered loss of business and had to pay wages …and buying flour for their customers from others. They took the matter to court for compensation for their loss

The wise Judge made the legal point that Baxendale's could only be made liable for losses which for foreseeable...the initial contract failed to mention the urgent nature of the delivery date. This landmark case still used today defines the limitations to damages for breach of contract

In the real-world contract law is complex. Corporate tax lawyers are among the best paid. With business involved in many contracts every day...they have now become standardized. As a former business owner, I have had to sign business contracts...a thorough understanding essential to know what you signing up to and its implications.

When dealing with big business the contract will always favour them...and they will have a legal department. However…my business insurance company gave me access to their legal department and free legal advice...i have used them on a number of occasions and saved money.

Literary censorship
All societies have laws against what is permissible in art... culture...music and literary works...restrictions on press freedom and censorship is prevalent in all societies

The reasons for censorship are for preventing the corruption of morals and ethics of society and prevent the public finding out unpleasant facts about their leaders. In the past obscenity laws used against D.H.Lawrence book 'lady Chatterley's lover and James Joyce book Ulysses...also the book Madame Bovary. The Church most active in bringing charges of 'outraging public and religious morals'.... the Church which supported slavery in the past... and the child abuse scandals among the Catholic church today

The problem with banning books is that it makes them popular with the public...they buy them to see what has been banned or being prosecuted for. The writer Salman Rushdie had a fatwa issued against him...which only made his book a best seller...he was stabbed in the eye by a religious retard...who's actions have only further damaged the reputation of Islam in the West

My advice...if you want to sell lots of copies of your book...offend as many people as you can...but make sure you're in a 'Police witness protection program' before you do.

Hang'em high...the death penalty
The death penalty...or legal murder is based on the Bible's 'eye for an eye'...that the punishment must be equal to the crime. However...the counter argument is that executions are a legal form of murder...or retribution. Venezuela was one of the first countries to ban executions...today more than 100 countries have banned state sponsored murder...however 50 countries still retain the death penalty...China carries out more executions than any other country

In the real world the argument has always been (1) its inhumane...murder for murder (2) if you execute an innocent person...you cannot bring them back to life.
In the UK the most famous case being a poor guy called Hanratty...he just happened to be in the wrong place...at the wrong time...with no witnesses to support his story

The Rules of war...to be ignored by the powerful
In past soldiers were the main casualties of war...today its civilians. The Geneva conventions of which there are four came about by a Swiss businessman called Henry Dunant...who was appalled at the death and injuries he saw at the battle of Solferino...Napoleon on the rampage.

He organized a meeting in Geneva…he managed to get the Europeans and the US to an agreement and the creation of the Red Cross...for the Israelis in Gaza to fire upon. They had another meeting at the Hague...the result ...the Hague convention ...to be ignored by the US and its Middle East Psychopath Israel.

In a Nutshell the convention is
1)Protect civilians...not likely...excludes the US and Israel

2)Protect prisoners of war from mistreatment and torture...excludes the US and Israel...for them this is normal practice

3)Repatriation of prisoners...excludes the US and Israel...they capture people and rarely release them...Israel has hundreds of children in prison...where is the moral outrage...nothing in the Western Media...all you hear is ...Hamas...Hamas...Hamas

4)Bombing and destruction of civilian infrastructure are war crimes...that is exactly what Israel is doing in Gaza with weapons supplied by the US…in Syria and Lebanon for decades

In the real world all the articles of the Geneva convention and the Hague convention…are broken...will be broken...and continue to be broken now...and in the future. The collective West if they applied the conventions…all their leaders would be prosecuted...including every US president since World War two for war crimes…in the UK Tony Blair for supporting the Iraq war on false evidence

The only people who seem to get prosecuted are African leaders...with the exception of Milosevic...the Serbian leader. Once again…the hypocrisy and double standards of the West on full display...while Israel carries out a genocide against the defenceless Palestinians in Gaza...the West is aiding and abetting Israel to carry out this Genocide...with the excuse its defending itself...from the illegal occupation of Palestinian land

The US Congress has passed a law that if any US citizen tried in the Hague ..they will invade the country to free that person. If the Hague wants to be taken seriously then it should try every Israeli Leader for crimes against humanity...the Palestinians who have suffered land theft and murder for over 80 years. The Geneva convention seems only to apply when the Collective West's interests threatened...i.e. the US and its vassal state the EU

The hypocrisy is in full display while Ukraine is given ..military...economic...humanitarian and diplomatic assistance...the Palestinians who are in the same situation are not. It makes no difference the majority world has seen enough and South Africa has acted...and got judgement...ignored by the US...Israel and the collective West...what hypocrisy

Genocide Joe Biden who does not know what day it is ...is not running the US ..he is senile...his handlers are running the show...whoever they may be. Every morning Genocide Joe Biden...his carers dress and feed him...they take him to work in vehicle with no windows...not to scare him of the traffic...when at the office he is given a stack of documents to sign ...which he never reads or understands.
He is kept away from the big red button with nuclear written on it...he has an evening nap...with his favourite cuddly bear

Then he is taken to a play area and given his favourite colouring book to keep him busy...while the State Department spokesperson lies on his behalf...and keeps the war machine going.

The Unions...sanity over profits
The history of labour unions is a battle of capital versus labour. The capitalist wants to exploit labour at the cheapest cost and labour wants decent wages and working conditions. The UK

was the first country to industrialize hence the first to have organised labour and unions and conflicts

In the past strikes were illegal in the UK

1)**As workers organized into unions** ...the government saw them as a threat...to economic stability

2)**The first strike was by weavers in Calton**...it was broken up by soldiers who killed six strikers...acts were passed to make strikes illegal

3)**Six farm workers 1834 tried to form a union**...sent to Australia...became known as the 'Tolpuddle Martyrs'

4)**In 1871 unions became legal**…but picketing was illegal...the Trade union congress formed in 1868

5)**1901 rail workers strike**...Court ruled union liable for disruption and compensation

6)**Unions join the newly formed labour party**…which when in office gave unions protected legal status

In the real world the Capitalist class has never made any real concessions to workers. These concessions have been bitterly fought over many generations. Today we have reversal… the Conservative party under Thatcher has greatly reduced the legal status and role of unions.

With global trade and global workforce ...companies have access to cheap...non-union...labour which they can exploit. With mechanization and technology fewer workers needed. However fewer workers mean more powerful workers.

My younger Brother was an I.T. Consultant...he could seriously damage by introducing a virus or other means and completely shut the company operations...there is no fool proof way of protecting your data…it is a constant battle to outwit the tech criminals

A while ago a man in the UK was prosecuted for digital crime...his virus software disabled your computer and you had to pay him to unlock your computer...he made over $500,000 ...and there are many like him all over the world.

Unions may be in decline but there many organizations all over the world which highlight using social media...companies which exploit workers...naming and shaming them...it works...especially with well know international brands...so much so that these companies have their own code of conduct on worker welfare...and no union needed

The Nordic Countries...law...welfare...prosperity
The Nordic countries of Sweden...Denmark and Norway have shown you can have a high tax...high welfare society...that ensures equality for all and no one falls below the poverty line

These countries in the past have had close relationships of mutual trade and social relationships. They have a similar legal code...as well as social and economic model...and it's worked for them...they have among the highest living standards in the world.

Due to their similar law codes they have been able to design and implement contract laws that are valid in all the countries.... this makes business and trade easier and less costly. They have gone even further in harmonizing a uniform legal system that covers...business...nationality...family law

In the real world these countries are 'City states'...with very small populations. The people themselves come from similar...ethnic...religious...and social background. These shared values have enabled the governments to have a cooperative political...economic and social model that works...because there is consensus

Today however with declining birth rates and mass migration to these countries...the social balance is changing with a more diverse society. Can their model survive...diversity does not mean unity...Multiculturalism does not work...this will be reflected in the Politics sooner or later

The Scandinavian people will soon be asking themselves 'who are we'. When everybody shares the same religion...culture...ethnicity. Social and economic values you do not question your identity
However when the nature of your society changes...especially if they do not like what they see...then identity Politics rears its ugly head...and labelling people as racist who question this ...is a good way to create racists and marginalize ordinary descent people...ask Mrs Duffy who was labelled as a 'bigoted woman ' by Prime Minister Gordon Brown...for questioning the high rates of Eastern European migration to her area.

How Japan became rich
Like many societies in the past Japan was feudal society run by the 'Shoguns'...they closed of Japan to the outside world...but did not stop economic and social progress. The strict internal laws and keep the foreigners out policy came under sustained pressure from the population who demanded changes. The Shoguns relinquished power and Emperor Meiji was installed...he presided over modernization of the country called the Meiji restoration

A new charter which gave citizens more rights...a parliament called the Diet...and opening the country to foreign trade. The conflict with America...and occupation by American forces...forced the emperor to announce 'he is not a living God'...however he is a dead one now.

Japan was forced to reorganize its political and economic system along the Western Model imposed on it. It became the second largest economy in the world...now however succeeded by China. Japan's rise is an economic miracle considering the destruction of the country by the US.

Cruelty to animals
Testing of cosmetics on animals and vivisection...i.e. using animals for scientific research has been around many years. However...cruelty to animal acts...and new strict regulations on vivisection have reduced the number of animals being tested

Alternative ways of testing cosmetics have been developed without the need for animals. Experiments on animals are still allowed but under very strict conditions. Animal welfare and animal rights have come a long way

Cruelty to tax payers
In most of the rich country's taxes have been rising...living standards declining. In France people were on the streets 'the yellow vest' demonstrations...people pay 50% tax and still cannot manage. In the UK taxes up to 50% and people are struggling

The tax extortion Mafia in the UK is taxing people to death...there never seem to be enough taxes. I am attempting to get a law passed...stop the cruelty to tax payers...we are losing our skilled and educated at an alarming rate as they emigrate...this cruelty has to stop...rising poverty and inequality and food banks for the poor.

Industrial injuries and benefits
In the past if you were injured or even died due to accident at work...there was no compensation or liability assigned due to negligence. The modern welfare state is a German creation under Bismark.

As Europe industrialized the number of accidents and injuries increased in factories. There was a need for some kind compensation or benefits for those injured or ill workers. In Germany a Socialist workers movement which later became a party agitated for a solution to this problem

Bismark who managed to unify the many states of Germany into one unified country was concerned that if this issue is not resolved it could become a dangerous Political problem...leading to unrest... passed laws which required employers and workers to put money into a compulsory insurance scheme

In the UK laws passed that a worker could get industrial injury benefit if he proved negligence by the employer. In America similar schemes...but their healthcare provisions are privately funded...also the US welfare system is far less generous than the European model...although once you reach retirement age...your healthcare is free and you get an old age pension

The problem is that in Europe with a population less than 10% of the world...it accounts for 50% of welfare benefits...this is not sustainable...many countries are having to make hard choices...either raise taxes...reduce benefits.... or do both...or import more migrants to tax as in the UK

When killing is justified
There is a very famous case of Boat which went a drift in a storm...after 20 days with very little food or water...two of the crew decided to kill and eat a third member who was in a coma. Later they were rescued and tried for murder in the Courts

The judge decided 'murder is murder 'regardless of the circumstances...no one has the right to take some one's life. They were given a very lenient sentence of six months...but a precedent was set killing a person no matter what the circumstances is against English law

In the real world all you need to do to justify murder is put on a uniform and you can participate in State sponsored murder of people in foreign lands...The US and its trusty ally Israel has been doing this for decades...ask the Palestinians.

You stole my land
Canada and the US was created by killing and disposing the indigenous people from their lands. The argument they did not own the land ...so we can take and privatize it. In Canada...the US...Australia and New Zealand the issue how to deal with land taken from the local people and compensate the descendants today...arguments still persist...no solution found to please everyone

Canada has acknowledged the wrongs and does recognise the land rights of the indigenous people...in Australia and New

Zealand it is still a very volatile political issue…. but they will never get their lands back

I do not believe there can be acceptable solution…as laws and society has changed…you cannot recreate the past and bring to the present...but some form of compensation in the form of enhanced welfare benefits might suffice...for a limited period...as with the Germans who have to compensate Holocaust survivors till 2030.

In God we trust...all else must pay
Monopolies have been around a long time in some form or another. In the US the issue came to a head...as oil was discovered … US Standard oil became a monopoly by destroying the competition by predatory pricing. In those days kerosene was used for lighting and as fuel for heating

Standard oil would drive out competition by undercutting the competition. The Sherman act forced Standard oil to split into seven companies known as the seven sisters. Trying to break monopolies is a tough task…the evidence needed is difficult to obtain and lengthy costly court proceedings. Governments use taxpayers' money to prosecute... court proceedings run into millions of dollars…if they lose the case…the state has to justify the expense.

In Europe the EU has fined US tech companies…the fines represent very little to the company's annual revenue…fining them 500 million euros of a trillion-dollar company...is laughable. The tech monopolies have now come to dominate our lives...there has to be a way of protecting customers data

How do you regulate tech monopolies when their company structure is spread over the world in different tax and legal regulations. The US has made a few attempts in splitting companies and giving space for competitors...the problem is the cost of entry is too high for most new entrants...the other issue is the US in public make statements against monopolies...yet actively supports its big tech companies from competition by banning l Tik Tok...on spurious security grounds.

Like most anti-monopoly acts they look good on the statute books...but ineffective and useless in practice...the idea that splitting a company ensures no collusion...or joint enterprise is beyond belief.

A well-known transport company in the UK used predatory pricing to destroy the competition...no less than 50 complaints made to the government about these practices...nothing done that could stop them...they are now one the largest private passenger transport companies in the UK...who says crime does not pay

Limited liability companies...not so limited
The need for limited liability arose because in the past a trader or investor...if losses occurred...he would be made liable for the full amount...the Ships carrying goods...if they sank due to bad weather...the trader or investor would be asked to compensate...resulting in bankruptcy or hardship

So limited liability was enacted to protect losses only to the money invested or shares owned...so if a company went bankrupt the creditors could only seize the assets of the business not the owners.

Like any good idea it has led to abuse of the system...fraud and embezzlement. Some owners would set up a new company...bankrupt the old company and transfer the assets to the new company and continue trading...known as Phoenix companies that rise from the ashes

More legislation to close these loopholes...only gives smart lawyers to exploit new loopholes created.

An accident claim company in the UK ...went bankrupt...the owner had taken out 'legally' $11 million dollars plus as salary...informed the 200 staff in the morning they had no job...he moved to Spain pictured with a... nice villa and boat...the law could not do anything to stop him.

Today however limited liability does not give 100% protection from creditors or the banks...they have their own rules and regulations which they will enforce on any business they deal with.

My advice if you are setting up a business transfer the house to the wife...make her a partner in the business...if things go wrong…you still have a house and a wife...otherwise if you lose the house ...you will also lose your wife...something serious for you to think about.

Remember in a court of law the most dangerous and damaging witness is your wife not the creditors...ask the former boss of GE electrics...his ex-wife destroyed his reputation in five minutes

Fire and death

Health and safety have never been a serious issue for capitalists. As the US and Europe industrialized...so has the number of work place injuries and deaths increased. Since big business control the politicians and ensure business friendly legislation...it took a terrible tragedy at the Triangle Shirtwaist factory in 1911...to high light how workers safety is essential

The factory employing mostly women…146 people burned to death...when the fire happened...escape routes inadequate...fire extinguishers not working...the fire brigade could not reach workers...their ladders not long enough...escape doors locked.

When the issue went to court the owners managed to avoid serious allegation of not protecting workers safety…compensation was very little…the owners were able to get the local politicians to support them...bribing the police to beat demonstrators. It took a new President FDR and the new deal to give workers better protection

It is a sad reality that only a terrible incident makes politicians to do the right things. The fire in a block of flats in the UK...where many lives lost. The whole affair turned from tragedy to farce as the owners...the council… the government blamed each other.

The owners said the installers at fault...the installers said that the council at fault as the flammable cladding was legal ...the council blamed the owners…as it was their building…a public enquiry reached no definitive conclusion…as each did not want to accept liability for fear of compensation which would run into $millions of dollars…in the end the tax payer and the existing tenants ended up footing the bill for this disaster

(Source:dk publishing the law)

The free market fantasy

It is normal for capitalism to concentrate wealth and power into smaller hands…that means cartels…monopolies…oligopolies. Governments have passed laws to prevent the concentration of business empires…like anti-trust legislation…in the US food and drugs administration FDA…in the UK anti-monopoly laws…mostly ineffective and useless…has not prevented the concentration of business

The effect of these legislations is negligible…big business can always find a way around any legislation. If a merger is seen as against competition rules…a business will find an alternative…like collusion or set up a new company not linked to the old one. All these legislations simply put up the cost of business to the consumer…raise the cost for new entrants…few successful prosecutions…if any…fines too low to affect the business.

To bring a new drug to the market can cost up to $800 million dollars in the US …due to strict regulations…result very few new drugs. If a struggling company cannot be bought out by a competitor…then it will go bankrupt with many job losses. In some industries 'size' matters in order to bring the price down for the consumer…economies of scale

It is far better to let cartels and monopolies operate as long as the customer gets goods and services it can afford…and the company profit margins are within the industry standards

Bill Gates operating system is reasonably priced…his office software is available free for students or heavily discounted…this is an intelligent monopoly that does not abuse its market power. This enables his company to come up with new innovative products rather than structure his business to avoid anti-trust legislation and tax investigations...which are time consuming and disruptive.

Catching criminals the hard way
The police need to follow the rules when apprehending criminals and charging them. Collecting evidence is tricky as criminals go to great lengths to hide their crimes...getting 'off 'on lack of evidence is common. Since the police have their 'hands' tied...some resort to dubious even illegal means to find evidence...house searches without a warrant is one way…planting evidence another.

If you allow a police officer into your house...without a warrant ...that is an invitation...laws have to balance the rights of people with the rights of the police to do their job...this is very difficult.

In the real world what this means is criminals are walking the streets who have committed crimes...but the police do not have the evidence to lock them up. The police attitude is if you are a habitual criminal sooner or later you will make a mistake and leave enough evidence for the police to apprehend you...and that is true...murders are solved very quickly ...while burglaries are not. It costs around $1 million dollars to solve a murder in the UK

The prison industrial complex is a money maker for the lawyers...courts...prisons...police...social workers...landlords...probation officers etc... except the victim...the cost of crime exceeds $50 billion in the UK…a thriving business.

Why give women the vote
Women in the past were not given the vote...excuses such as they are less intelligent or too emotional to vote. There was a concerted and consistent activism for reform with little success

The change came with the first world war when millions of women recruited for the war effort working in factories doing 'men's' jobs. Since women were now actively participating in the economy the reasons for them not to get the vote became untenable…Women finally get the vote.

In the real world ...the West with its high morals and enlightenment could not give equality or votes to women...this shows the gap between public statements and the reality. Women were paid less than men in the UK...it took a long struggle with legislation eventually passed that gave women equal pay

What this shows that any improvements in people's lives have been bitterly fought for and bitterly resisted. With Neo-liberal agenda now sweeping the world...many of the worker rights and protection are being eroded. As an example in little old England there are now in law zero hours contracts

What this means in practice is you are not given fixed hours to work...so if you work for a supermarket...they will give you a four-hour slot during the day to work...so you become a prisoner in your own home...you cannot leave in case you get called to work...this is inhumane and cruel...yet legal

From Russia with love

Russia was an internal empire ruled by the Tsars. The peasant population was exploited with little material or social progress. The issue came to a head where people demonstrated for change only to be set upon by soldiers... many killed. A massive peoples led revolution took place headed by Lenin

His intention to get rid of the ruling elite and monarchy and replace with worker councils and worker coops. A new constitution was made to reflect the new realities.

Lenin did not live long enough to see through the reforms...he was succeeded by Stalin...a paranoid Psychopath...who was disastrous for his country...leading to mass starvation...unbelievable cruelty against anyone who challenged his authority.

After Stalin the country did industrialize in the 1960's where people's basic needs were met...however this economic system was not to last...again another popular people led revolution defeated Communism...and there is now liberal plural democracy in Russia and rule of law

The history of Russia tells us how laws are made...they reflect the changing power structure and dynamics of the country. So…laws were not made to protect people's rights but to protect the power structure against the people

Right now… we see this at work in Pakistan...the country is ruled by the US backed military dictatorship…with fake democracy and rigged elections. At this very moment the popular support for Imran Khan's party… PTI party is being reversed by massive vote rigging...prepared ballot boxes being introduced to reverse the actual result...so that the Military's preferred party wins

The constitution and legal system is being trashed...the police used as a para-military force to arrest people on phoney fake charges. The rangers another para-military force… another arm of the army used to suppress and quell public dissent. Complete disregard for people's rights as written in law...Judges who are compromised...handing out judgments which are not based on 'law'

As I write the election results are being delayed to allow for the massive vote rigging...mobile communication turned off for short periods…including the internet...censorship of the mainstream media. Results announced before votes counted. I fear the people who know what they voted for...if results not fair and accurate is going to lead to social unrest...i see lots of anger on the streets

With social media and the rise of independent journalists...people have access to the truth and know what's going on...nobody watches or believes the national TV channels...their low viewing numbers reflect this. The young here are use social media all the time…WhatsApp is very popular here...50% of the population under 25 years old.

With very high mobile phone usage here people have access to information...concerning the political and economic situation of the country. The rule of law has yet to settle in Pakistan...despite the constitution giving people rights...they are not protected in practice. A colonial era law used to arrest people without warrant or evidence...complete abuse of the legal system...yet judges here do not question these practices.

Unfair treaties
As I have stated before laws are made by the rich and powerful in society...that applies to countries as well. The first world war was started by France and Britain...as they feared German industrial power. The war went badly wrong for France and Britain and the defeat of Germany came about with the support of the US.

The Versailles treaty which Germany was forced to sign was imposed on a devastated and bankrupt country...it lost its coal mines...land...reduced army and had to pay reparation of billions. It gave rise to Hitler whose main aim was to reverse the treaty and rebuild Germany...which led to World War two

Had the treaty not been so onerous and had people listened to John Maynard Keynes...who expressed great concerns over enforcing a treaty which Germany could not afford. Sixty million people lives could have been saved ...and most of Europe would not have been destroyed...what madness and stupidity of the political leaders...happy to send other people's children to die for them

My solution if politicians vote for war...their children must be sent to the front line first...this will end all wars to end wars

Duty of care
Customer care in the past was not a high priority for the capitalist class. However... an incident of a person drinking ginger beer from opaque bottle containing a snail in a cafe was to make legal history for which we are indebted.

The drinker sued the cafe owner...the court ruled the cafe owner has a duty of care for his customers to ensure they are given safe food and drinks while at the premises. However…since the owner could not have foreseen the snail in the bottle…he was not liable but manufacture is.

This landmark case has given consumers immense legal rights…as a former retailer if a customer is harmed or injured from a product bought from me...they have full legal rights…and compensation from me...even if the manufacture is at fault…in this case the customer sues the retailer and the retailer sues the manufacturer.

The business community have made it difficult to sue them...the cost of litigation…the evidence needed...the bar is set very high...so most cases never get to court...outcome is... out of court settlements which are a fraction of the money that could have been claimed

When you hear cases of high court settlements where large sums of money awarded…these are usually very rare ...unusual cases...with special circumstances.

The right to bear arms and murder people
When the US constitution was formulated…there was a provision for the people to have access to arms. The reason for this was to protect the country from invasion by Britain and it was a very lawless country at that time

The mass shootings every year has not deterred the arms industry or the legislators to ban or restrict arm sales...so the murders continue. There is no genuine reason why Americans need arms...it is the world's leading military superpower. Water pistols have been banned in certain states…but not weapons that kill

The powerful gun lobby has been very successful at watering down or stopping any restrictions or bans on weapons. The documentary film maker in his film… Bowling for Columbine ...went into a bank to open a new bank account…they gave him a shot gun and bullets for opening the account over the counter.

The gun culture in American society…in films and the language and is pervasive...leading to a militarized society...hence the high rate of gun violence. My solution replace lethal guns with paint guns...at least the violence will be more colourful and less deadly.

The new world order
The historical nonsense about the first and second world wars… I will not go too deeply into...only to say history is written by the victors. Every 'actor' in World War one and two has blood on their hands...including the Jews...the Allies... the victims and perpetrators

European history is one of wars...ending in the two most destructive wars ever fought on European soil. To avoid such future events the UN was created and later the Geneva convention…the creation of the EU and the convention on human rights.

The UN is not a world government ...it has no army to enforce its judgements...a tool of Western imperialism...the convention on human rights excludes the rights of the Palestinians...these laws are applied selectively when Western interests threatened...Israel is committing genocide in Gaza and all the West is doing ...should we send more arms ...and which leader to send to Israel to kiss Netanyahu's 'ass' and ask him to be more humane in the murders he is committing.

The new world order is very much like the old-world order…Western Imperialism...business as normal...funded by the tax payers of these countries.

Nuremberg trials...the victor's trial
The Nuremberg trials which are seen as humanities stand against genocide...were nothing more than a sham trial… a victor's trial. The victors had to try the German command for crimes which they themselves committed. The indiscriminate bombing of German cities by the allies killing thousands of people

in each bombing mission were war crimes…as well as bombing supply routes for civilians

To overcome the charge of doing the same… which was a charge made by the German officers...new laws were made to try the Germans and exclude the allies of the same charges.

As for the Jews and 'holocaust' I suggest the reader go to the holocausthandbooks.com and read lectures on the holocaust...free to download. According to them the conventional holocaust narrative has more holes than Swiss cheese and sinking faster than the Titanic.

The six million holocaust figure has been reduced to below three million and the numbers go down each year. At the Nuremberg trials the holocaust witnesses were never cross examined...whatever statements they made was taken as fact...their statements were often contradictory. No witness has actually seen a person being gassed or can describe the gas chambers in detail…no witnesses were cross examined to test their stories

A retired Judge after reviewing the Nuremberg trials...came to the conclusion that most of the defendants could not have been convicted on the evidence provided...which was hearsay...not actual physical evidence...basically a sham trial...a victor's trial...not to be used for teaching law students

Since the trial was rigged from the start many of the defendants were beaten or tortured...others killed themselves taking cyanide. Today the West prides itself in promoting and protecting human rights...yet failed to do anything to stop the genocide in Rwanda.

Trying the Serbian leader for crimes against humanity...while ignoring the fact once NATO decided to support one side ...atrocities increased as a result ...and the bombing campaign ...which caused huge amount of damage and loss of life...may have contributed...Western Hypocrisy and double standards at their best

If international law means anything...if applied then every US President since the second world war would be hanged for crimes against humanity...the over 50 countries that have been invaded...over 20 million killed...the $billions of dollars in destruction and damages...land theft and stealing of resources.

If International law applied today then we would be invading Israel and trying the Prime Minister for genocide...So if international is to be taken seriously it has to be consistent and applied equally...dragging African leaders and not anyone else makes a mockery of the law

The UN and the International court...for entertainment purpose only
It is far easier to make laws than enforce them. The UN...its Charter and the International court of justice came after the second world war. The UN was designed not to work when those on the security council can veto any suggestion put before it...we see this with the US veto any proposal for a ceasefire in Gaza.

The General assembly where the world gets to vote...its decisions are not binding...its peace keeping function only works if there is already a peace...it does not have means to bring peace to a region. As for its other missions too little money to make much difference to world poverty or bring peace...love and happiness.

What this organization is... a 'career enhancement' organization...if you work for them you can put on your CV for future employment. The countries who have succeeded from being poor... to being rich like South Korea have done so by themselves. People put too much faith in these organizations and we should see them for what they are...empty monuments...talking shops...words are cheap...actions are costly

The UN convention on the rights of the child...a wonderful document...come to Pakistan where child labour is prevalent...and nothing is being done...empty promises never be fulfilled. If the rich countries are so concerned...why don't they get together and fund poverty alleviation programs...or better still write of third world debt

The UN declaration of human rights has around thirty provisions …I will list them here taken from 'the law book 'by dk publishing...see how many your country manages to implement or avoid: -

1)All humans equal and free...only on paper...not in reality

2)Free from discrimination with rights...not if you are Julian Assange

3)People have the right to life...liberty and safety...not if you are a Palestinian in Gaza...the world's biggest open prison

4)No one should be kept as a slave or in servitude...there over25- 40 million slaves in the world today

5)No torture or inhumane treatment...unless you are in an Israeli jail as a Palestinian prisoner ...or in Guantanamo Bay

6)Everyone has right to be recognized as a person ...unless you're a stateless Palestinian

7)The law should be the same for everyone...there is a law for the rich and the rest

8)Everyone should have right to help… to protect their rights...that is if you can afford a lawyer

9)No one arrested or exile anyone without good reason...in the UK you can be arrested for looking suspicious…in Pakistan you can be arrested without warrant or evidence

10)People have right to a fair and impartial trial...ask Imran Khan...former Prime Minister of Pakistan with over 200 fake and phoney charges against him...he is now in jail

11)Everyone is innocent until proven guilty...that is until the Police beat a confession out of you…or fabricate or plant evidence

12)No one should attack a person's privacy or reputation...ask the Palestinian surgeon in the UK arrested after talking about

Palestine on the media...the police arrested him ...using the terrorism act

13)People have freedom of movement in their own country...if you can afford to move.

14)Everyone has right to seek asylum abroad...welcome to the UK...thousands of 'refugees' turn up on small boats...now being housed in hotels...while we have a homeless problem

15)We all have the right to a nationality...unless you are a Palestinian...then you are stateless

16)Men and women can marry and have children...in poor countries lots of children

17)All people have the right to own property...if you can afford it...for many in the UK ... unaffordable

18)Freedom of thought is everybody's right...in the UK we have hate speech laws...which mean anyone can feel offended ... can make a complaint and the police will investigate...a woman outside an abortion clinic arrested for a thought crime ...later released...when the police made to look like fools

19)People have the freedom to opinion and expression...not so you can be silenced or shutdown...by social media...the mainstream media or the government...censorship is everywhere

20)Everyone has the right to peaceful assembly...only if the police permit it

21)Government authority must be based on free elections...not so in Pakistan...where elections are rigged

22)Social security must be provided where needed ...only if people pay taxes and governments are not corrupt

23)All people have the right to work and fair pay...not if you work in a Bangladesh garment factory...or in a sweat shop working 12 hour shifts for a pittance

24)Everyone should have leisure time and paid holidays...does not apply to the above

25)Food and shelter are basic rights...for many in the world not affordable. Malnutrition…starvation and hunger

26)Education is everyone's right...if you can afford it…or the government can provide it for free

27)We should protect artistic creations ...not sure what this means

28)All freedoms should be available world-wide...universal freedoms yet to emerge...work in progress

29)We have duty to protect other people's rights...not sure what this means...if no one cares about my rights...why should I care about other people's

30)No state or persons can take away these rights...rights are taken away all the time by state and non-state actors

In the real-world people's freedoms and rights have come at great expense of their freedoms and rights...Apartheid South Africa suffered many if not all the above mentioned. Countries pick and choose which of the above freedoms they will implement or ignore

The UN human rights provisions can contradict with other countries laws ..customs...social values...or traditions

Sharia law being one such example. All the Human rights declaration is good for is putting in books ...monuments...and posters...and talked about

The EU superstate created its own human rights charter...a cut down version of the UN declaration of human rights...it does allow EU citizens redress in the European human rights court...there judgements are legally binding and enforceable unlike the UN

However not all EU countries have been accepting of some of its rulings…especially when it comes to dealing with migrants and asylum seekers...each country pushes the problem onto another

Greece which is an entry gateway to Europe…simply registers them and moves them onto another EU country...the Italians put them on coaches and send to the UK…a soft touch country...as do the French giving migrants time tables for trains and trucks for them to board while they look the other way

Hence the UK voted out of the EU...only to end up with six million plus Europeans seeking British nationality...while the UK is now importing migrants from the rest of the world...only for migration to increase

The United state of Europe
The EU originally designed as a trading bloc with a trading currency ...the Euro...had this remained it would have worked...but the EU clowns have decided to create the United States of Europe...by ever increasing integrations with never ending series of legislations here is the outcome of this meddling:

1)The European court of justice…found guilty in your own country... you can take your case to the European high court…convince them that your human rights have been violated…despite being convicted of rape and murder...and get a release date...then sue your country for compensation

2)The elected EU parliament is a joke...the people who run the show are unelected bureaucrats...not answerable to the electorate

3)The treaty of Paris...states give up power to the EU clowns

4)The common market...no longer common...dominated by mega-corporations...the treaty of Rome...more power to EU clowns

5)European atomic energy community...to develop EU energy security...they did this by blocking cheap Russian gas and oil...only to buy from a third party at inflated prices

6)Now we pay up 5x times for LNG from America and elsewhere...after they blew up Nord stream 1...just to make sure Europeans will make American LNG suppliers super rich

7)The treaty of Brussels…more power to EU clowns and the European parliament...for entertainment purposes only

8)The Maastricht treaty...more power to EU clowns…if you vote no… another referendum will be held until you say yes...send in the clowns

9)The Helsinki treaty...don't want to join the EU fully...we will create a special club for you to join...for the Nordic countries...you get the benefit of the EU and tell your citizens your independent...what a joke ...this is back door entry to the EU
10)You get to join NATO the US European military alliance and threaten Russia...a country with more nuclear weapons than the US... this should give you sleepless nights

11)In the real world the EU clowns attempt to create a political and Economic rival to the US and now China. It will not work...with over thirty countries with different cultures...history...politics…legal systems

12) Different Languages...traditions…laws. There is no such thing as a European citizen other than you live in a Geographical area called Europe

In every EU election…more and more EU anti-EU candidates are elected...yet the EU clowns take no notice of this...continue to waste taxpayers' money...on wines lakes and butter mountains...as it subsidizes its farmers...while promoting free trade.
(Source:dk publishing the law)

The doomsday machine
The father of the atom bomb Oppenheimer...near the end of his life ...described himself as the destroyer of worlds...he died a

tortured genius...knowing full well that human existence can be extinguished in less than one hour...by nuclear weapons

Attempts at limiting nuclear proliferation have been a failure...Israel and Pakistan are recent arrivals on the nuclear scene. The Lunatics at the Pentagon believe they can win a 'nuclear war'...using what they call tactical nuclear weapons which would unleash death and destruction in a limited area.

Twice we have come close to nuclear annihilation...the Cuban missile crises being one...i will not go over the nonsense written about this...the USSR did not back down...a secret agreement was reached that the US would dismantle or withdraw missiles from Turkey (a NATO country) ...and the USSR would dismantle its missile basis in Cuba.

A US navy commander was given instructions to arm the nuclear missile launchers...he refused...later it was found out it was false order...A similar thing happened to a Russian Commander...he also refused the order. Thanks to these two people I am able to write about this...they should be given a 'save the humanity award'

Nuclear weapons do not act as a deterrent...it only encourages countries to acquire them... a parity of terror...known as mutually assured destruction known as MAD. Nuclear treaty bans and bans on testing has not reduced much the number of nuclear weapons and it will not do so...because Weapons inspectors need full access to nuclear facilities...Israel has always refused...no one can force them to comply

The treaty of non-proliferation of nuclear weapons is endorsed enthusiastically by the countries who have nuclear weapons. A treaty can only be applied if the countries agree to abide by it...ratifying it is only a commitment to do so...lots of countries are committed to it but few want to implement it 100%...putting your country at risk by reducing your nuclear deterrence is a vote loser.

Either all countries have nuclear weapons or no country should have them

Now the US and USSR have reduced their nuclear stock piles…it does not make the world safer. Imagine you are in a room with Petrol up to your knees...to light it you only need one match...having a box of 12 matches does not make any difference...the one match will see you burn.

When countries make a big show how they are making the world safer by reducing the number of nuclear weapons...or banning testing...does not make the world safer...only nuclear disarmament is 100% safe. Even without a nuclear war the world is heading for ecological disaster...it may take a little longer...the outcome will the same...end of civilization

Civil rights and Black power
Even though the US constitution gives equal rights to all citizens...but not if you were Black. As i said before it is easier to make laws than change people's attitudes. Segregation remained in the US mostly in Southern states...with Jim Crow laws

It took more than Rosa Parks to refuse to give up her seat… to get rid of them. The momentum slowly took of that these blatant injustices must be got rid of. The civil rights movements organised all over the country by all members of society...black and white including politicians and people from the entertainment industry

Public support and the organised demonstrations and the law was used to end the injustices. Now however the issue of Race still plagues America...the Black lives movement...the beating of Rodney King...the trial of OJ. Simpson and other such incidents...show that biased attitudes still exist in American society...laws do not change people's attitudes...that has to come from within...But also Race should not be used as Political weapon or excuse for immoral…unethical...or illegal behaviour

In the real world the way these laws to protect minorities can have untended consequences. In the UK we have race relations laws to protect minorities...and anti-Semitic laws to protect the Jews. What happens is that these laws end up persecuting the majority. A case in the UK where an Ethnic minority brought a case against his employer for discrimination. The case had no evidence...but the employer paid as it did not want adverse publicity

Another case of anti-Semitism against an author critical of Israel by Zionist Jews in the UK...the case was investigated and rejected. By bringing such baseless cases the effect will be to diminish these laws...juries and Judges will become 'case hardened'

My suggestion get rid of these laws and use civil law...where you only have to convince the local judge...which is easier than bringing a criminal conviction where the evidence needed is much higher.

The right to remain silent...is the right to commit more crimes One of the bedrocks of the Western legal system is the right to remain silent. The idea it protects one's civil liberties and the crimes you may have committed. In other countries if you refuse to answer questions it is seen as an admission of guilt.

It is right that people rights must be protected against arbitrary arrests and the Police implicating you when there is no evidence...i.e. Police corruption...which is a clear and present danger. So legal safe guards are necessary.

In the UK and US Police now have body cameras which can record evidence or interviews...this is a very good idea. In the real world in the UK when a potential criminal is apprehended and interviewed and they are asked questions ..the most common reply is 'no comment'.

When I was a retailer one of my customers job was to transcribe these 'no comment 'interviews into a paper form for the Defence...the Courts...the prosecution and for the Police record. She said it was the best job in the world ...all she needed to do what type 'no comment'

However…the criminals may not be winning by remaining silent. Body language experts can review interviews of a serious nature and can determine whether the suspect is lying or not. This gives the Police information whether to prosecute or not.

The British legal system is regarded as one of the best in the world and the one of the most expensive. The Judges are corrupt free and independent and take the law very seriously. The bar needed for criminal convictions is set very high. The Crown Prosecution service better known as the 'Criminal protection service' is more concerned with saving money than prosecuting criminals. There have been many cases where insufficient evidence has set perpetrators free...not good for justice or the public

Tiger Moto solution
The legal system and justice have parted...we must bring them together again. My suggestion is when suspects are apprehended...they must be fully informed of their rights. The interview should be filmed close up...the suspect must answer...their lawyer or independent witness must be present.

All the evidence must be presented to the suspect. The filmed interview must be viewed by a body language expert.

The defence and prosecution must work together to determine the guilt or innocence... and all evidence must be presented to the jury…including all previous convictions...otherwise you have the situation where a rapist was set free...once the jury found out about his previous rape convictions...they were in tears knowing they had set a guilty man free.

The above system works in Germany…France and Spain...where all evidence including previous convictions are considered. The Police in the UK take the attitude that habitual criminals will be caught...sooner or later…when they will make a mistake and give the Police enough evidence to prosecute them...they also know who the criminals are and what crimes they commit.

Public safety must be paramount otherwise trust in the Police will decline. By bringing in what I call 'flexi-law' were all the evidence is considered...the circumstances...previous convictions...and any other factors relating to the case...by the prosecution and defence working together. This way the suspects rights are protected...the legal system is open...fair and transparent...and Judges should be given more investigative powers...rather being 'referees' in the court room.

The UN Political rights charter
This is another meaningless document that countries sign up to and few will implement if their national interests threatened especially American interests...once again here is a list of things which you can decide if your country abides by or not:

1)Freedom of religion...persecution of religious minorities is rife

2)Freedom of expression...the censorship in the mainstream media and elsewhere is rife...at the moment the mainstream media in Pakistan does not report the arrests...vote rigging...beating of protestors before and after the elections

3)Right to assembly means being beaten and tear gassed in the US...pepper sprayed ...corralled into a small area in the UK

4)Right to fair trial...not in Pakistan...over 200 fake cases against Imran Khan ..former Prime Minister...or Julian Assange

5)Freedom from torture...unless a Guantanamo prisoner...where you have no rights or in an Israeli jail...where torture is routine

6)Discrimination on the grounds of
race...gender...language...religion...this happens all the time

7)No discrimination by social class...can anyone believe this does not exist in every country...we define ourselves not what we have in common ...but what makes us different...social class being one

8)Right to vote in free elections...not in Pakistan…US backed military dictatorship...fake democracy and rigged elections plus corruption from top to bottom

In the real world the US and EU will use the above charter to persecute countries or their actions they do not...as a way of interfering in the Politics and economics of these countries…linking trade...investments or loans with conditions attached as above.

If the collective West really cares about the above I suggest they:
1)Get rid of the rigged trading system keeping these countries poor

2)Stop stealing their resources

3)Write of the debt which these countries cannot afford

4)Stop the looting and laundering of stolen money from these countries...the City of London...the world's leading money laundering centre

5)Stop funding and arming terrorist groups like ISIS

6)Stop selling arms to these countries and fuelling conflicts

7)Give equal voting rights in the UN

8)Free and fair trade...means getting rid of farm subsidies… stop regime change when these countries elect leaders you do not like

9)When some or all of the above is done then we might see a better world.

The Divorce business $50 billion in the US and rising Divorce was once considered shameful in society...making couples stay together when... they no longer liked each other was also shameful. In the past when divorce was difficult or impossible...many couples were married but separate...since divorce was socially undesirable.

The collective West introduced no-fault divorce a ludicrous idea...since fault should be apportioned. Judges have often said that divorce is not their business...the way they deal with it is like a commercial transaction...the women with children get the house and maintenance from the ex-husband

A very bad deal for the husband. In the US the divorce business is worth $50 billion per year. As a former retailer I have met many divorced customers who tell the same story...in law they have no rights or representations...the whole court system is in favour of the women

My business neighbour who is divorced for many years is still fearful...his ex-wife will often pass his office to see what car he is driving. If she see's new car she will go to court to demand higher maintenance...to avoid higher payments he drives a beat-up second-hand car

This is the state of the divorce business. In the US a millionaire business man has set up his own YouTube channel to help men get a better 'deal' in divorce court proceedings...his main advice is to get divorced in a state more friendly to husbands. He also gives advice on the kind of women to avoid. In the UK there is 'Fathers for Justice' trying to fight for better deal for ex-husbands and partners.

Their main concern is that court maintenance payments are paid direct to the mother and visiting access to the children. On the issue of payments…they say they will pay directly for whatever the child needs...but there is no way they can be sure the money paid to the mother will be spent on the children

As to the visiting access to the children...mothers will come up with all sorts of excuses to deny the father access. One of my customers was asked by his daughter she needed $400...when he questioned her it was the mother's idea...she needed the money to go on holiday with her new partner. Another customer ended up having to send his mother to collect the children on Saturday from a local supermarket car park…as he had been banned from visiting the house

In another case...the divorce settlement was the wife gets the house...he continues to pay the mortgage and maintenance for his daughter...once the house is paid...he will only get 50% of the sale of the house when the ex-wife decides leave

The trend is divorce is rising as countries industrialize...this means more divorce lawyers…a career for you to consider... a very lucrative business.

The witness protection program
This came about to protect informants especially those who testified against the Mafia...in the US...a violent dangerous parasite on American society. The program has been very successful at considerable cost to the US taxpayer and not one informant has been killed in revenge attacks.

I think this program should be expanded to include other groups...whistle blowers who reveal corrupt practices in government or business. People who divulge corporate tax dodgers...should be protected

People like Julian Assange with Wikileaks...which tell the public the underground workings of the deep state...hidden from the public view...how their tax money funds wars...land theft and murder in distant lands...all in the name of Democracy and Human rights.

The Abortion debate...both sides are right
For most of history women have been treated as second class citizens...often treated as property. Before contraception pregnancy could have serious consequences...having a child out of wedlock...or abandoned by the father...or disowned by her family...there were also health issues...women dying in child birth and other medical complications

Abortion was illegal in many countries...the Catholic Church a strong opponent...hence why the Irish use to have large families...there was an Irish family i knew...they had seventeen children...Irish women use to go the UK to get an abortion...because of the ban in their country...even today the abortion debate is polarising society and reflected in the Politics. No Politician will openly be pro-abortion.

With the Church and the general attitude that women are inferior...getting abortion was going to be an uphill struggle. Two things in the sixties brought about change (1) the contraceptive pill (2) roe v wade which made abortion legal in America...women's movements for equality in the sixties and the changing status of women entering the work place on equal basis...reflected in the Politics.

The anti-abortion group say that abortion is murder...life begins at conception...the counter argument is that abortion within the time limits set… is terminating a pregnancy...not killing a child not yet born. The pro-abortion camp say that a woman has the right to choose as it's her body.

Women have resorted to 'back street abortions. Most countries have sensibly passed laws which is a middle ground... (1) abortion permitted within time limit... (2) if beyond the time…have the child and give up for adoption... (3) if woman's health at risk...or the baby...or product of rape...permitted (4) if all else fails you can still get an abortion in another country…if you have the money

Roe v Wade in the US has been overturned making abortion illegal...however not many states are enforcing it...the arguments and debates continue

Tiger Moto solution
In the UK it is estimated that 40% of pregnancies are unplanned...what is the point of bringing a child into this world unwanted…uncared for...it is better to have an abortion. If a woman gets pregnant then a guarantor must be provided in case the husband or partner is unable to support the child...my guess both sides of the family will be made to sign a contract

Since the guarantors will be obligated legally...they may take a keen interest who their children pick as partners...if not suitable they will have veto power and the girl or boy has to decide can she go it alone financially

Now before you start to criticize me this already happens in many non-western societies.

In Singapore when a woman gets pregnant…they have to go to a government department and provide guarantors in case the couple split or unable to provide for the child...usually both sets of families...or future grandparents. The governments rational they do not want children unwanted and uncared to be looked after the state in orphanages

In the Islamic world the father-in-law is the guarantor in case the relationship fails...also there is contract which stipulates the compensation to be paid for the divorce. The advantage of this system is since the family is involved in choosing a suitable partner for their boy or girl…the risk is shared

In the majority world in 70% of marriages the families are directly involved...marriage is seen as a commercial contract with a 'element ' of love...unlike the collective West ...the 'love' business is destroying their societies...and high divorce rate is proof… i come from a background where to get married is a very serious business...my two sons are married and very happy
In order to get married they have to be vetted and approved by the girl's family…every aspect of the boy's background...friends...age...qualifications...career prospects and income are closely scrutinized

Once you have been approved engagement follows and a marriage date set...which will cost both sets of parent's immense amount of money...costs of weddings $30,000 plus and rising...marriage is seen as an investment where both sets of parents provide a good start for the couple

When i was a retailer a young medical student...a customer of mine from a Muslim background...was lucky she found a suitable partner…once approval was given by both sets of parents ...they were engaged...the deal was... once she qualified...her parents pay for the wedding...the boys' parents pay for a deposit for the house...she gets to choose the house

Species extinction
This has been going on since humans learnt to hunt…first we hunt for food ..second we clear areas for agriculture and living. In the past when populations were small the damage was insignificant...today however it is reaching critical point

The US and EU have passed legislation to protect certain species and habitats ..in the rest of the world the species are losing out badly. Protecting a few species like the bald eagle in the US or newts in the UK hardly makes any difference to species extinction...in Africa the animal life is on a fast reduction program...the lion and elephant population is declining rapidly

The real threat to species extinction is not animal life but the human extinction which is now distinct possibility. As the population is expected to hit 10 billion...we are rapidly reaching the point of no return...as we hit resource limits. It is impossible to give every person on the planet Western living standards…. we would need two planets

Since we do not have a world government and every country acts in its own interest...we cannot save the planet...it will exist for another 500 million years...the human race will not last that long... many people are calling this period we live in ...our last century.

The 21st century...our last
We live in the best of times and the worst of times
1)Many diseases have been conquered...over use of antibiotics has made new strains of diseases resistant to antibiotics

2)The hole in the Ozone layer...a thin layer that protects the earth from lethal radiation is damaged…someone must repair it

3)Life expectancy is rising...as is education and poverty is declining...high population growth and urban density of population is putting considerable limits on resources

4)New diseases like the Covid…spreads fast in high density populations

5)Climate change refugee's abandoning their countries and heading for rich countries

6)Cloning humans is now possible...this raises many ethical issues…do you want many copies of you wondering the planet

7)DNA testing and crime...data protection and privacy issues

8)The high divorce and separation…leading to destruction of the traditional family...in the UK ...in future the average family will consist of unrelated parents and children.

9)The threat of nuclear annihilation is with us...the US constantly threatening Russia and China ...may lead to a final war to end all wars

10)Rapidly ageing populations...means decline in workers and pension providers

11)The internet...digitization...mechanization...is making many jobs and professions redundant...unemployment may become a way of life for many people...how do we deal with this coming problem

12)Mass migration mostly from poor countries to rich countries…. barriers to migration going up...people do not want their country flooded with people who do not share their social values…. ethics...religion…. liberal democracy ...this only leads to conflict as people vote anti-immigrant parties…and labelling them as racists…only inflames the issue

13)The above are a small number of problems humanity has to confront...the big ones are climate change and global warming and mass migration...the UN is dumping refugees on to poor countries...where they are not wanted. Algeria is getting flooded with African migrants...it has a local black population of 10%.With mass migration this may double...as well as the resentment...including against those already settled local nationals.

How Chemists win wars

The use of chemical weapons during the first world war such as mustard gas...caused death...disability and excruciating pain and agony. Japan also used them against the Chinese...in Iraq used against the Kurds. The use of chemical weapons is now banned...however enforcement is the real issue. The danger of chemical weapons is always with us...how to destroy and make safe existing chemicals...especially if you do not who has them and in what quantity

The WTO...the biggest con job in history

The WTO... the World Bank and IMF are US creations to control world finance and trade...sold as a win-win for humanities benefit...is the biggest lie...the workings of these institutions show their intentions...to impoverish the majority world and to lock them into dependency to the West.

The WTO ensures free trade between nations ...has the power impose fines and sanctions on countries who flout its rules. In practice its judgments are weighted in favour of rich and powerful countries who can afford the expensive lawyers to represent their interests

When I did my useless Social Science Degree...the WTO rules were described ...as countries were price takers or givers...work this out yourself. Let's look at a real example...a US company has been dumping cheap chicken parts on Haiti...destroying its chicken market. It applied to the WTO...the ruling were in its favour...Haiti cannot sanction or impose tariffs on US business

The WTO rules are ignored all the times ...or selectively applied against economically weaker countries...the EU continues to impose high tariffs...despite WTO rulings...The US will use the

WTO to further its own interests...and use bilateral trade agreements to overcome any WTO rulings it does not like

The WTO cannot ...and will not…cannot ever give a level playing field for trade and investment...since every country or trading bloc will always find a way around any WTO rulings it does not like. The US has been imposing high tariffs against China despite providing no proof that China has been subsidizing its industry or using spy technology in its products

As the world's biggest trading bloc emerges and a currency for its trade...the BRICS countries are going to directly challenge the WTO...the IMF and the World Bank and Western hegemony...get ready for war...stock up on essential supplies

Test tube babies and the sperm bank
This is another issue that is never be resolved...scientists believe embryo research is needed to cure diseases...at what point is an embryo a human being...the pro-life say it's at conception...we all started as embryos to adulthood...it's a process...if you intervene at some stage of the process…you are committing murder. Others see the embryo as a collection of cells read to propagate into a potential human being

The science lobby have had partial victory...they can experiment on embryo's under very limited and strict circumstances...others see this as a 'fudge' as state sanctioned murder. My neighbour when doing his PhD in science had the opportunity to investigate some embryo's...his experience has definitely turned him against abortion...you can watch on the internet… a painful to watch abortion where the foetus is 'chopped up' and withdrawn from the female

This video should make people think...and practice 'safe sex'.We are now at the point where sex is separated from reproduction...abortion on demand...women can have children without needing a 'man'...welcome to the world of the sperm bank and test tube babies

If babies are not a product of a 'loving couple' but a consumer item today...which women can have any time...you also have gay couples fathering children...surrogacy is on the rise...rent a womb...in countries like India…as long you have the money…it's all legal

Tiger Motto's Advise
Now by destroying the traditional family structure are we heading for a better world...imagine you're are a child raised by two 'mums' or two 'dads'…parents evening is going to be interesting plus the ridicule you will suffer at school...you are guaranteeing yourself emotional and psychological problems in the future...my advice get hold of the contact details of a good Psychologist

The right to know who the sex offenders are in your district The terrible crime of rape and murder of seven-year-old Megan Kanka...led to legislation for people to know if sex offenders 'operate' in their district...the offender had been convicted of similar offences twice and served time… was released to commit more crimes

The people who released him need to provide an explanation...you cannot cure a child sex offender...their sexuality is imprinted on them… that they are attracted to children...very difficult to change. The effect of this law is no one wants a sex offender living in their area

There have been cases of people taking the law into their own hands and inflicting punishment...a case in the UK …a man was wrongly accused had people at this house threatening him to leave the area

Monitoring sex offenders is a complicated...time consuming ...and costly business

I cannot see a sensible solution to this problem...the case of Robert Black Britain's worst child rapist and murderer has destroyed 'childhood'...responsible for up to 14 child rapes and murders...although only convicted of a small number of crimes...he still haunts parents today

Copy right protection in the age of the internet...a fool's paradise

When copyright laws were introduced, there was no internet or mass communication. The concept is to give the owner time to make a profit from his invention...book...music etc. Today with file sharing so much stuff can be accessed for free...and also the dark web

Governments have passed legislation to stop music piracy...but it has been pointed that those who download music for free are most likely to buy legitimate copies at a later date. With millions of people downloading illegal software or music ...how are you going to stop this and punishing potential buyers does not make good business sense.

YouTube does try to stop use of copyright materials...all that means it ends up on another digital platform...the copy right laws are out of date...the free stuff or 'creative commons' is destroying the old copyright system...books are a classic example ...you can legally read or upload 30 pages of any book… can be digitized and sent over the internet.

Tiger Moto Advise

Get rid of copyright laws...give stuff for free and charge the user for updates...it works...whenever I download free software, I always give the owner $10...since the copyright owner does not need to go to the expense of copyright or patent protection...that person can make just as much money from voluntary donations

The creative commons are the future...there is an inventor who will give a microchip free ...i.e. at cost of production with a small profit...the chip can do most things… in a kettle or washing machine. It is not a high-end chip...but will serve for most ordinary functions...and it can be programmed…he still makes money and has a thriving business model for others to emulate.

The US is very concerned as they own a lot of the world's most important patents and copyrights...they are trying to create legislation to curb copyright theft and deal with the 'creative commons'...i believe it's a losing battle...they are up against the 'collective intelligence' of the world community online...good luck to them...they will fail...welcome to the new world order...and it's not American or Western

Landmines... a cheap way to kill and injure people
Land mines planted during conflicts around the world are still killing and injuring people today. The people who supplied these are the major arms suppliers of the world...they are cheap to make and very profitable

The arms suppliers should be made to get rid of them...or if anyone injured, they must pay compensation to the victims...if they were to do so… the arms industry would be bankrupted...which would not be a bad thing

Giant rats are used to sniff out landmines and explosives...the good thing is they can be paid in food only. The US is the world's leading military power and arms manufacturer and supplier to many conflicts around the world ...as well as directly involved in many conflicts around the world...the Middle East being a classic one.

There is no stopping the US military machine ...and the lunatic Giant rats in the Pentagon who run it… these people from the US military should be forced to sniff out landmines like their giant rat counterparts…this will make them think seriously before engaging in conflict…just like forcing Politicians children to serve in the front line of any conflict

Lots of agreements…lots of talks...a little money which will not solve the problem...landmines will still be used in the future…but will have 'postcodes' attached to them for later retrieval if unused

A drugs free world
Recreational drugs uses and abuses are part of youth culture in the West. Criminalizing drugs has not reduced drug use only to

fill the prisons with people whose only crime is to have the 'wrong type of weed' on them

The US being the worst offender with its brutal legal system...its war on drugs an absolute failure...the rational being by preventing supply the demand will cease...backward thinking by a society obsessed with a puritanical streak inherited from the religious crackpots who first settled in America. Reduce the demand for drugs by better education and supply will cease

In Europe Portugal is the first country to decriminalize all drugs...it has seen a dramatic reduction in crime...and deaths related to drug addiction. This lesson is yet to be discovered by other nations. I have a personal interest in this matter...as I lost a brother to drug addiction...he got mixed up with the wrong 'crowd' violence...lying...cheating...stealing...to fund his drug addiction...criminality became normal to him

All it does is make drug dealers rich...a drug gang were convicted in the UK...they were making $12,000 dollars per week...they ended up owning 30 properties...drug addicts have to steal $ thousands of dollars to feed their habit. By making drugs legal...the cost savings are huge ...the cost of drugs is minimal...it would get rid of the criminal element...and reduce crime substantially

When it comes to recreational drugs sensible rational discussion does not exist in the UK. To illustrate this a cartoon once appeared in a serious newspaper...it showed two cartoons...side by side (1) a fight in a Bar...too much alcohol in people (2) in another a group of adults quietly sitting smoking cannabis...while outside the house a gang of Police waiting to bust the house

When it comes to recreational drugs there is more 'heat' than 'light'...the stupidity and insanity continues...endless discussions that get nowhere. No Politician wants to be seen soft on drugs...a vote loser...hence the social problems continue...and no solution in site...more waste of taxpayers' money

Gay rights

Gay rights are a minority issue given far too much importance than it deserves. Homosexuality has always existed...even though it is forbidden in many religions and banned in some countries...gay rights is a peculiar Western phenomenon...the rest of the world simply ridicule this… to them an absurd notion…not worth discussing

When Western countries try enforce their social values against other countries...as with Russia…they quickly meet resistance...there will be no gay parade in Moscow...as the gay-lesbian mafia was to find out.

Giving gay and lesbians equal rights is one thing...but 'gender bending' where a person 'chooses' to be recognized as male or female is going to extremes…biology determines gender and to a very limited extent ...a social construct…i.e. how you act…behave and dress…you are either born with male or female parts…the lucky ones may have both.

There is a terrible case in the US where a separated dad is taking his wife to court. The issue they have a child less than 10 years old who is a boy by biology…his mother has decided he is a girl…it is obvious this child is a boy…his mother is subjecting this poor boy…. to child abuse…I hope the Judge takes the child of this demented mother…and gives to the father…so he can have a normal childhood…as a boy

As a former retailer I have confronted this issue. A customer of mine...adult male who worked in the building trade…decided he was a 'woman' trapped in a 'man's' body

He went to see a psychiatrist...who's consultation was there was nothing wrong with him other than he had an unhealthy obsession to dress in women's clothes. He then went to another Psychiatrist and managed to convince him he had a serious problem. He had an operation to get rid of his wobbly bits...had his nipples pierced

The result is… he has lost his job...lost his family...his neighbours are not too keen to talk to him…has long hair…wears dresses... and has a small dog as a companion. He was in bar once...decided to use the women's toilets...female customers complained…told by the Manager to use the other toilets ...sued the bar for discrimination…. received $6000 compensation...and got himself banned from the bar

Not only is the West trying to overturn three million years of human evolution…with trans-rights and gender bending...the rest of the world do not see things the same way...they have fixed gender identity and gender roles in society and they intend to keep it that way...because it works...so the gay-lesbian mafia need to be aware trying to enforce your agenda on other societies will not work…. remember no gay parades in Moscow

(Source:dk publishing the law)

To die or not to die

Mercy killing...helping a person to die is moral and ethical mine field…like the abortion debate both sides have compelling arguments. The mercy killers say it is wrong to prolong a person's life who is terminally ill...in agony...or is so disabled to the point…that person is a living corpse with no quality of life...and sustaining these people serves no purpose than to prolong the agony

The no mercy killers say it is wrong to take a life under any circumstances...people should die naturally. However…the legal status has changed under extreme and unusual circumstances with consent from the person...a person may be permitted to die…Switzerland is the first country to make mercy killing legal...so people can go there to die and no one will be convicted of murder

In the real-world Doctors make decisions on mercy killing every day...patients who have reached to point where medical science has reached its limit…treatment will be issued with a DNR notice…that is do not resuscitate

My 86 years old mother ended up in Hospital with Pneumonia the Doctors said they will give her initial treatment ... a DNR notice issued before treatment...luckily...she recovered only to die six months later from kidney failure

Crimes against humanity...why the US is never convicted
The ICC or international criminal court...another well intentioned useless organization...is to make money for international lawyers...and convict leaders from third world countries...the ICC investigates

War crimes exclude the US ...they can commit as many as they like...they can carry on murdering people around the world in the name of democracy and human rights...no court can stop them

Genocide...excludes the US and the Middle East Psychopath...Israel...which is committing genocide against the Palestinians

Crime of aggression...excludes Western powers...all murders they commit are legitimate

Let's look at the workings of the ICC ...Rwanda and Yugoslavia ...Ethnic cleansing ...which could have been avoided with early intervention. Very few people prosecuted...with Yugoslavia the Serbian leader being prosecuted died in prison...the trial estimated to have cost $millions of dollars

Most of the people tried have been African leaders...it is seen by the majority world as Western imperial institution...they point out Tony Blair and George. Bush should be tried for war crimes...illegal invasion of Iraq on false evidence presented at the UN and the House of Commons

When will Israeli leaders be tried for land theft and murder for over 70 years in Palestine...the West right now is funding and supporting economically and diplomatically the genocide in Gaza...hypocrisy and double standards...applying international law selectively makes a mockery of the law. Passing judgement is one thing...enforcing it is much more difficult...when the West has the best legal teams and money...to avoid any indictments

The Junky Olympics

Every four years athletes assemble to compete who is the best in the world. There will be more drug cheats at this event than in your neighbourhood. As humans reach the physical limits of their sport ...performance enhancing drugs may be the only way to win...this is like an arms race

Testing for drugs is now mandatory...the problem is the cheats are usually one step ahead of the drug testers. Now there are drugs that mimic the bodies normal hormones...insulin is very popular among body builders and strength athletes...keep a close eye on the next Olympics and try to spot the drug cheat

Tiger Moto advice
Legalise drug taking and let's see how far athletes can go

...they will reach a limit to what the human body can endure...once that limit is achieved and all athletes will produce the similar results...they can all be winners…. lots of gold medals

The climate can change… we will not

Here is a list of international climate change agreements...which many countries signed up to ...and have no intention of honouring 100%:

1988...IPCC

1992 Rio summit

1992 Kyoto protocol

2009 Copenhagen summit

2015 Paris agreement

In the real-world countries happy to implement those measures that do not affect their economies negatively. The UK has set emissions targets...the only way to achieve this is to subsidize green energy. The solar panel business the payback period is in excess of 20 years and electric vehicles…which are far too expensive to buy. Canada has stepped back from some of its commitments

The climate continues to change and CO2 emissions continue to rise...since we do not have a world government getting compliance is a real issue. Rich countries imposing their own environmental standards on majority countries will not work...they cannot afford them and it deters development

Match fixing...winning by losing
With sport now big business...the temptation to rig matches is always there. In some Asian countries gambling is a 'national sport'...the Chinese have a 'gambling culture'. There exist gambling syndicates that are actively engaged in bribing sports people...cricket being one sport

There have been some well-known cases of corruption in sport. The problem is hard to detect... sports people do not always win...bookmakers now use sophisticated software to detect unusual transactions...such as when a large amount of money is put on a sports outcome just before the game finishes

Data protection...not for the NSA
With the rise of the internet the issue of privacy of data has highlighted a fundamental problem. The EU forced google to delete unwanted data...the case of Spanish man who did not want his personal data to be seen on the internet

Google complied with the ruling by cancelling the link to his information...but google argued the information is still out there and accessible

Since there is no universal law to govern the internet...a country may pass any law it wants to protect the privacy of its citizens...enforcing on the internet is an impossible task

Since internet providers are only a digital platform...they cannot be made responsible for content...which is what the EU ruling is trying to do...banning or putting restrictions on internet access will deprive EU citizens of information which may be of use or value to them

When YouTube censors or deletes content...it ends up on other digital platforms like rumble...Tik Tok...Facebook...X. In fact... banning things which are not illegal.... creates a market and encourages competitors...which is what YouTube is facing...and google by censoring content...gets people to use DuckDuckGo...which does not…or Rumble.com

Governments need to be made aware they cannot control the narrative by controlling the main stream media...as the internet will quickly expose their lies...they cannot control the internet...they need to be more honest with the electorate

Even the Chinese government cannot control the content despite its best efforts to insulate the population...in a digitally global world censorship does not work. The real threat to the internet and privacy issue is governments can force internet service providers data on its citizens

The internet service providers well know by doing so it will lose trust among its subscribers...this will impact on their business model...encourage competitors. As an example, the swift system run from Belgium ...controlled by the US government ...is used in money transfers

The US government has blocked Iran and Russia from its use...the effect is there are now four emerging money transfer systems competing with swift. The spying organization called NSA in the US...monitors internet traffic on the excuse to prevent 'terrorism'...which is interesting coming from the world's biggest terrorist state...the US. Most of the information it collects is used to persecute its own citizens...nothing to do with terrorism

Tiger Moto advice
If people want privacy there should a body set up where they can register ...not to have information about them on the internet...but they cannot be selective...that means no information about them will be available of any description…permanently

Net neutrality if you can pay for it
He who controls the internet controls the world…with information the new 'oil ...control and access to the internet means huge profits for corporations and spying opportunities for governments

The first issue is the internet a commercial enterprise or a public good...something we all rely on...i believe it's a public good and net neutrality is essential to ensure commercial interests do not override public interests

This debate has become very heated in the US...with freedom of speech is the freedom of the internet. You have big corporations trying to strangle their competitors by slowing or restricting internet flows...by control of isp's

In Pakistan where I am writing this book...the government is constantly interfering with the internet...some days very slow speed...other days no internet for hours or days...with so many businesses use the internet ...economic damage to business interests is being done. When asked the government uses the excuse...there were 'technical issues' with the internet...no one believes them

The public supports net neutrality...big business and governments do not. The internet is fast becoming an alternative political...social and economic platform for people. Governments see it as a threat to their authority while big business see a threat to their profits...with so much free stuff online

Information is education...education you have to pay for in most countries...if it's free we can all benefit...it's only a matter of having internet access. By seeing the internet as a utility...controlled by no one...owned by no one ...not regulated...that does not mean that illegal activities should be allowed...we can all benefit

Politicians are control freaks...they like to control the political narrative...i.e. their lies must be protected...the internet exposes their lies...using terrorism as an excuse to control what's on the internet will not work...as wise Judges will see the fraud perpetuated on the people and will protect people's rights...so politicians beware...trying to control the internet is a vote loser

Tiger Moto Advise

An independent news outlet (the Gray zone) ...based in the US has been very good at exposing the lies of governments and politicians in the West. One of its reporters while visiting the UK was detained by the Police under the terrorism act and asked a lot of questions for hours...he was later released with no charge

A world expert on the Middle East Illan Pappe while visiting the US was detained at the airport and asked lots of silly questions. When he asked on whose behalf he was detained for and why…he was given vague answers like from the State department or national security issues. The real reason was he is a critique of Israel and the powerful Israel lobby wanted him detained

Here we have a law designed to apprehend terrorists used against a law-abiding citizen to harass them and silence them...this what politicians do in Banana republics. The UK government is behaving the same way...who asked the police to arrest and detain these people...no justice…no law...no protection…like the Palestinian Doctor arrested and not charged

The net is a public good...must be protected and allow citizens free access...big business should not use it to extort excessive profits...if they do… ban them from the internet...or transfer their operations to competitors...governments should not use it to spy on their citizens...the net should be legal but free...There must be international laws to ensure it is free from manipulation by big business and governments

The internet is far too important for any one government to control...it is the future...the digital world is here to stay
Equal pay for all...but not all paid equally

Women in the past on average would be paid less than men. Equal pay legislation has forced employers… equal pay for men and women doing the same jobs. However… the pay gap still persists...the reasons are complex:

1)Women are more likely to work part time due to family commitments

2)Women may work in industries where traditionally pay is low...like retailing

3)Women opting out of work to have children...means when they go back to work...the job title may have changed...lower pay

4)A Woman may turn down promotion...taking on extra responsibility with a little extra pay may not suit her

5)Careers choices...professions such as teaching or nursing...where pay is low

6)Where women who do reach high profile positions in public or private life…either have to get other women to look after their children or will leave to look after their children...former boss of Pepsi Cola did this

7)As a former retailer I paid my male and female staff equal pay...the female staff worked part time...due to family commitments

Tiger Moto advice
Equal pay for equal work should be the norm…legislation ensures this...however men and women pursue different career choices...this is reflected in the different pay structure...i.e. they end up being paid less. Secondary school teaching in the UK over 80% of teachers are female...it is a low paid profession

Now working women are not necessarily all single or low paid...many will have partners with incomes…since women are responsible for 70% of house hold spending...if you add the partners income to theirs...they are no longer classified as low income:
for women
Equal pay for women = less pay = + partners income = more pay
(Source:dk publishing the law)

The law in summary

This chapter on the history of law is very important…without a proper legal system...that protects your individual freedoms and property is essential. In countries where rule of law does not exist...like Pakistan…Police can arrest people without warrant or justification and bring fake...phoney charges against them

If Peoples property rights are not protected...there is land grab going on in Pakistan where poor farmers are having their land seized for development and they are not benefiting...if they complain they are locked up for years in prison...too poor to employ a lawyer to defend their interests

UK law…turn the victim into the perpetrator and turn the preparator into the victim…there is in the UK the Moron support industry of social workers…probation officers…Psychologists…the legal system etc who support and justify criminal behaviour and make money from it. Labelling bad or criminal behaviour as a mental illness …and excusing the perpetrator for their actions

The law has to be just...accessible to all...and work...i.e. equal before the law. Most of the laws in the past were made by the rich and powerful in society...to protect their interests...namely land and property. This is why in the UK most of the laws are still property based

The rich and powerful are not immune from criminality themselves...so the law has to be flexible enough for them to avoid prosecution. In the UK this means…the bar for criminal convictions is set very high...it ends up protecting the criminals more than the victim...the Crown Prosecution service is known as the criminal protection service...let me explain by a real-life example

My son when age 12 years old had a 'paper round'...one day he was delivering newspapers in the neighbourhood on his bike… a gang of 15 years old youth put a knife to his throat and stole his bike

We informed the police …who told us we know who the culprits are but we do not have sufficient evidence...as they are under 17 years old the… full force of the law does not apply...as they are treated as 'minors'...have child protection laws

This is the sad reality of how the legal system works in the UK...it's not the Police at fault…they want to lock up the criminals...it's the do goodie politicians passing laws to protect people's rights...only to end up protecting the rights of criminals ...or would be criminals...if you as an adult touch a child regardless of the circumstances ...you can be prosecuted and end up with a criminal record

Here is another example...one of my customers was a maths teacher...he had a particular problem with one 15-year-old girl...she consistently failed to do her assignments…he told her that if she did not complete her assignments…she will not pass...she told him that if he insisted ...she would inform the school that he was sexually harassing her

He immediately informed the Head teacher… who informed the police and parents of the false allegation…this is what happens when you make in law 'rights of the child' as opposed to 'rights to the child'...rights come with duties and responsibilities…again our do goodie politicians responsible for this mess

Many schools now make parents sign a school charter which has strict conditions on what rights the child has while in school...if you don't sign the charter…your child does not go to that school...the Charter is a good behaviour charter…designed to get rid of unruly children...i.e. bullies and Morons...which are a unique feature of British schooling

One of my customers an English teacher…worked in South Korea His experience their ...this society has a learning culture…students turn up on time…ready to learn… homework completed and returned on time. Very few behaviour issues…bullying or thuggery… trouble makers evicted very quickly from the school premises...no return policy for the child

Miscarriages of justice are a common feature of the British legal system. In high publicity crimes like murder the Police are under intense pressure to solve them quickly. What happens with no serious evidence or lead to the perpetrator… the Police will find a suitable social inadequate to pin the blame on.

This poor person of limited intelligence will end up confessing to a crime he did not commit…often evidence withheld of the persons innocence from the jury to guarantee convictions.

In majority of low-level crimes like burglary the conviction rate is less than 10%...car theft and street crimes are rampant…the Police instead of dealing with crimes...simply records it and give victims a helpline number of a victim support group...who offer tea and sympathy…British style

Serious crimes like rape the conviction rate is less than 10%...so in effect the British legal system is a criminal's charter…if you an aspiring criminal please come to the UK …you will do very well…with little chance of being caught

It appears the best Legal system in the world can deliver the worst outcomes…. welcome to UK law…to be avoided…if possible…at all costs …otherwise it will cost you all you have…and no justice

Tiger Moto advice
If possible…avoid the British legal system...it can trap you into a never-ending legal procedures ...which can be costly and time consuming. This is my experience with the British legal system...justice and the law parted a long time ago

Even if you win a legal case and get judgement in your favour...enforcing the judgement is not so simple ...if the loser disappears. There are nearly a million county court judgements which have never been enforced. The UK's out of date legal system…is still out of date...over 800 years old and does not deliver justice…but makes plenty of money for the legal profession

US law...plead guilty and get a reduced sentence

The US legal system is brutal...people can be given long prison sentences for minor crimes. Since it is private money-making industry. It needs a steady supply of inmates...to keep the prison industrial complex profitable

Recreation drug users and the black community are a particular target and with the US gun culture it is inevitable when there are more fire arms than people...violent crime becomes normal. The right to bear arms was passed to protect the new country from invasion by its old colonial master...little Old England. Today it means murder and mayhem

A person will be prosecuted for a crime...given the option admit to the lessor crime and you will get a lighter sentence...refuse and if convicted you will get a lengthy sentence. The logical outcome...people admit to crimes they are innocent of...the conviction rates make it look better than it is Overall crime has not come down or deters future crime...but makes money for the prison industrial complex and lawyers

Japanese Justice

In Japan lying is a criminal offence...applied in the West would mean most of our Politicians will be locked up. However...they have one of the highest conviction rates...mainly due to confessions.

The way it works ... an arrested person is continually interrogated...until they confess...guilty or not. They also have what is called hostage law...by apprehending a person for theft or other 'money related crime'...the person is kept in prison until the family or others come up with the release money.

Many Foreigners end up in prison in Japan over what would be regarded as minor crimes in the West. Theft is taken is taken very seriously regardless of the amount of money involved

Law in the Gulf States

The law is not independent of the Rulers...if you are a member of the ruling family...you have immunity...if you are a local…you will be treated leniently…however if you are non-local…depending on the type of crime committed you are at the mercy of the courts

In Saudia Arabia criminals who burgle people's homes…before leaving will often sprinkle the place with alcohol. If the theft is reported… the Police will be more interested in the alcohol than the crime… you will need to do a lot of explaining…hence many burglaries not reported

Every day Korans are dumped in sewers in Saudia Arabia. This action has very severe consequences for those doing this… a person was executed for allegedly ripping up the Koran and flushing down the toilet

The people doing this are obviously protesting against their rulers…as there is no free speech and criticizing the Monarchy is not allowed. If caught these people will face severe punishment for desecrating the holy Koran and the birth place of Islam…Mecca

The EU Laws...rights to everybody …responsibility to no one
The EU clowns who run (ruin) the EU …have developed a comprehensive legal system to protect human rights. The result is it gets to interfere in laws of other countries…criminals can now get their lawyers to take their cases to court and get judgements overturned

Rather than protecting people's rights...which is a good thing…like the British legal system also end up protecting criminals who use it to their advantage…with endless appeals and judicial reviews…it becomes a money-making racket for the Lawyers and the purpose to give justice… gets lost in legal wrangles

The issue of illegal migrants entering the EU is one such disaster…each country tries to pass the issue onto other countries. Hungry…a small country cannot cope with the high levels of migrants entering it borders… by putting barriers at its borders…it falls foul of EU laws…and gets fined for not complying with EU law

The EU is a shambolic enterprise designed to fail...the EU clowns are trying to create the EU in their image...i.e. liberal...Tolerant...diverse...cosmopolitan ...a borderless world...with happy go lucky residents. The reality is there is no such thing as an EU citizen or a common policy on Political and economic issues.

With 27 countries in the EU...the idea that you can have a common policy on anything is remarkable. Everybody in the EU wants the benefits but not the downside of enforcing EU rules...among the worst offenders being Hungry and Poland. The other issue that its accounts are never fully ratified...it seems to be a constant work-in-progress never to be finished.

The colossal waste of money in creating an EU bureaucratic Empire controlled by the US...with EU taxpayers money funding this doomed enterprise. I am old enough to remember the original concept sold to the public was that there would a great EU trading area with the Euro as the trading currency with consumer protection...and there would be visa free travel in the EU

There was no mention of people from other countries claiming benefits in your country...or compete in your labour market...border controls would remain...a countries own currency and laws would apply.

The Politicians lied to the public about the true intentions of the EU project...now people know and vote in the EU for anti-EU candidates...if these get voted in great numbers ...they can form a political block and make the EU un-workable by blocking legislation

The EU support for Israel is undermining its credibility as genuine supporter of Human rights and rule of law...that nasty little country called the UK has been doing its best to protect Israel at the international court. The double standards and hypocrisy .... hallmark of the West...are in full display...the majority world has taken note...and pointed out the double standards... this has not changed the Western mind set.

Tiger moto advice

Stay away from the law or become a Lawyer. In most countries the law does not deliver justice. In the UK the law is game between the defence and prosecution… the judge as Umpire…with endless legal arguments while the legal bill accumulates

Sources

DK Publishing: the law

Joshua Rozenberg: your rights and the law

Rawls theory of Justice

The Economist Magazine